To Turn the
Perfect Wooden Bowl

The Lifelong Quest of Bob Stocksdale

Masur birch, Russia, 1993,
4½" x 4⅜" (112mm x 111mm).
Collection of Forrest L. Merrill.

To Turn the
Perfect Wooden Bowl

The Lifelong Quest of Bob Stocksdale

by Ron Roszkiewicz

Fox Chapel
PUBLISHING

To Turn the Perfect Wooden Bowl: Bob Stocksdale's Lifelong Quest is an original work, first published in 2009 by Fox Chapel Publishing Company, Inc. No part of this book may be reproduced in any form or by any means, electronic or mechanical, without written permission from the publisher.

Unless otherwise noted, all photos by Ron Roszkiewicz.

Unless otherwise noted, all bowls by Bob Stocksdale. Material, creation date, dimensions, and current owner included when available.

ISBN 978-1-56523-388-1

Library of Congress Cataloging-in-Publication Data

Roszkiewicz, Ron.
To turn the perfect wooden bowl : the lifelong quest of Bob Stocksdale / by Ron Roszkiewicz.
    p. cm.
ISBN 978-1-56523-388-1
1. Turning (Lathe work) 2. Stocksdale, Bob, 1913-2003. I. Title.
TT201.R66 2008
684'.083--dc22

2008043402

To learn more about the other great books from Fox Chapel Publishing, or to find a retailer near you, call toll-free 800-457-9112 or visit us at *www.FoxChapelPublishing.com*.

Note to Authors: We are always looking for talented authors to write new books in our area of woodworking, design, and related crafts. Please send a brief letter describing your idea to Acquisition Editor, 1970 Broad Street, East Petersburg, PA 17520.

Printed in China

First Printing: January 2009

Because working with wood and other materials inherently includes the risk of injury and damage, this book cannot guarantee that performing the activities in this book is safe for everyone. For this reason, this book is sold without warranties or guarantees of any kind, expressed or implied, and the publisher and the author disclaim any liability for any injuries, losses, or damages caused in any way by the content of this book or the reader's use of the tools needed to complete the projects presented here. The publisher and the author urge all woodworkers to thoroughly review each project and to understand the use of all tools before beginning any project.

Dedication

To my darling Phyllis: I hope you like it.

"Every time I needed a fix, I would go see Bob and
buy a couple more bowls. He was an inspiration
for me, and I was always amazed at how he could see
what was inside of a log before he cut into it. He did
miraculous things with those bowls that he made, and I've
always been a big promoter of Bob."

—George Saxe, one of the premier collectors of
    contemporary crafts in the United States and a benefactor
    of the new Dorothy and George Saxe Gallery at the de Young
    Museum in San Francisco's Golden Gate Park.

Amboyna, Malaysia, 1999,
3½" x 8¼" (86mm x 209mm).

Contents

Foreword
The Father of American Woodturning

More than just a fellow woodworker, Bob Stocksdale was an inspiration to me and a very good friend. I believe the first time I met him was at the first Conference of American Craftsmen (in 1957), sponsored by the American Craft Council. It was held at Asilomar in Pacific Grove, California[1], and I recall the majority of the attendees were ceramists. When we broke up into small groups, there were about 10 woodworkers—a group that included Walker Weed, Art Carpenter, and Bob—and we all became good friends. After the conference, Bob and I talked on the phone at least every other week. I remember him as a free spirit and a very straightforward man. He either liked you or he didn't, and he let you know it.

Bob was both a woodturner and a businessman; he made bowls primarily to sell, and he worked five days a week. Though he may have had to struggle at first, from the time I knew him, he was always able to sell his bowls. I once asked him if he kept a record of the bowls he made. He responded that he didn't know what was so important about keeping a record. Bob's prices were high for those days—$50 for a little bowl.

As an artist, Bob's style wasn't to make the great big bowls they do now. Instead, he was a very utilitarian turner whose bowls were made for use and not just to look at. In choosing wood for his bowls, Bob had an eye for wood that had a nice pattern in it. I often bought wood from Bob because he always had a whole garage full of wood. I'd see a piece, and he'd say, "that'll make one, two, three, four bowls" in order to price it.

In addition to being Bob's friend, I'm also a collector of his bowls and have quite a few. A piece in our collection that my late wife just loved was a 24-inch (609-millimeter) salad bowl with straight edges. It still amazes me how he was able to turn down to one-sixteenth of an inch (1.5 millimeters) and make a bowl that is 24 inches (609 millimeters) in diameter.

As far as I'm concerned, Bob Stocksdale was the father of American woodturning. I think that without him knowing it, people were influenced by him. He was one of the very first and the best. He was the heart of what people are doing now in woodturning.

Sam Maloof

December 2008

[1] **Editor's Note:** There is some indication that the first meeting between Maloof and Stocksdale took place at the Los Angeles County Fair and not the ACC Conference as Maloof recalls.

Introduction

To Turn the Perfect Wooden Bowl: Bob Stocksdale's Lifelong Quest began in 1987 while I was working as a consulting editor with book publisher Charles Scribner's Sons in New York City. It started out as a personal quest to uncover the enigma that is Bob Stocksdale—something I had done with other craftsmen during my previous eight-plus years as catalog director at Woodcraft Supply.

By 1987, Bob was one of the last of the top-tier craftsmen who had not written a how-to book or hit the summer workshop circuit. Having known of Bob as a craft icon, I was curious to find out if he was as proprietary as he seemed about his methods, was making a success of his work, and had lessons he would share with others about making a life in America as a cultural anomaly.

At that time, the woodworking and woodturning renaissance had been well under way in the United States for at least ten years. Many books, videos, and magazines on these subjects were widely available. Mail-order companies were selling a range of turning tools, and training courses were popping up all across the country. This wealth of choices was in stark contrast to the 1960s and 1970s, when only a few books and a handful of tools were available—even for professionals. At that time, the only two turning books were from British woodturners Peter Child and Frank Pain. Unfortunately, neither book provided the comprehensive instruction necessary. There were no videos, of course, and the only mention woodturning might get in magazines was in support of a lamp project in *Popular Mechanics*. Of course, there were professional artists and craftspeople plying their trade at the edge of the cultural radar. A few, Bob being one of them, were collected and celebrated and achieved national and international reputations.

The objective of this book—now as it was at its inception— is to provide a snapshot of a few days in the studio of an American original and to hear him describe his life and work in that comfort zone. The Bob Stocksdale I photographed and interviewed at his home studio in Berkeley, California, was open and generous with his information and seemed to appreciate that this was an opportunity for him to express his thoughts and opinions in one relatively brief, concentrated period of time. He was patient as we set up the photographs. The stories he told were of a pure American journey. As a part of the day-in-the-life theme, I photographed work-in-process pieces from the drying room and finished items that were ready to be sent out. I borrowed some exotic Japanese papers from his wife, Kay Sekimachi, to use as backdrops when photographing the tabletop images.

Black walnut burl.
4½" (112mm)
x 4" (102mm).
*Collection of
Jerry Glaser.*

Black-and-white photographs and audiotapes were recorded in parallel with the process of making the bowls and platters. The book text is taken directly from the transcriptions of the audiotapes and maintains Bob's Midwestern drawl and idioms. The result is an incomplete portrait of a life in craft from the mouth of one who not only survived but also thrived in it. The techniques he used are still relevant but admittedly not easy to explain through words on a page. His thoughts on marketing, pricing, and other related subjects were given with a twinkle in his eye.

Through his simple but masterful way of working, he showed us there is no need for exotic mechanical chucking devices or an array of tools of every shape and size to shape wood. Over the years, he developed techniques to suit the tools he had and was able to achieve excellence, inspire scores of turners who followed, and supply museums, galleries, and collectors with objects that enriched their lives through elegant forms and the natural beauty of wood.

I was to learn during my week following him around that he was too busy supplying his customers with bowls to bother with writing books or teaching. He was keen, however, for my book to get published and perhaps raise even more the visibility (and prices) of his work. I did my best to spark conversation into as many areas as I could without getting in the way of his narrative.

This book was originally planned in 1987 as a Scribner's imprint. The editor-in-chief, my mentor, Jacek Galazka, thought it would make a worthy addition to a new special-interest book department planned by the company. Unfortunately, Scribner's was bought by Macmillan, and then Macmillan was the subject of a hostile takeover by Robert Maxwell, and both the special-interest program and the Stocksdale book were killed in their infancy. The materials languished on my shelves until I brought them to the attention of John Kelsey at Fox Chapel Publishing. The result is the book in front of you.

The first editor of this book, my wife, Phyllis, passed away in 2003. She organized the data and transcribed the audiotapes in 1988. The very readable version we now have is the result of the work of editor Gretchen Bacon with management from John Kelsey of Fox Chapel Publishing. Thanks to Alan Giagnocavo, president of Fox Chapel.

Bob's wife, Kay, was patient and supportive of my questions and requests and provided numerous materials. Collectors Forrest Merrill, Jane and Arthur Mason, Dorothy and George Saxe, and Norman Anderson were supportive and helpful. Photographs from M. Lee Fatheree were made available through Jill Berk Jiminez of the Berkeley Arts Center. Finally, thanks go out to David Ellsworth, Albert LeCoff at The Wood Turning Center, and Sam Maloof for taking time to summarize their relationship with Bob over the years.

Bob passed away in 2003. He was 89 years old. I hope Bob, somehow and in some way, can take pleasure in the fact this book finally is being published and at least some of his story is being told.

Ron Roszkiewicz

July 2008

African blackwood.
5" (127mm) x 7" (176mm).

Bob Stocksdale sharpens a
chainsaw blade.

Biography:
The Origins of an American Woodturner

During his life and after his death, woodworker and woodturner Bob Stocksdale was and is known as a master in his field. His trademarks were his use of simple tools and exotic woods and his appreciation of wood's natural beauty. This section traces his life and features some of the many newspaper and magazine articles that were written about him and his work.

Though he focused on bowls, Bob also turned other items. Shown here are two walking sticks, one plain and the other ornate, made by Bob. Both are made of snakewood. The bottom one measures 34" (864mm), and the top one measures 36" (914mm).

A close-up view of the turned and inlaid knob of the ornate walking stick.

Born in 1913, Bob Stocksdale spent many of his childhood years in Huntington, Indiana. His father, a dirt farmer, had about 280 acres, pigs (which they slaughtered for food), and some cows for milking. Bob lived on the farm with his mother, father, three brothers, and one sister. The Stocksdales' life was not an easy one, but it wasn't in Bob's nature to complain.

Bob's interest in woodworking began when he was six years old and his grandfather gave him a pocketknife. He spent time whittling birdhouses and was very good with his hands. By the time he became a teenager, during the Depression, Bob had set up a woodworking shop in the barn. His first lathe was one he built. Because the family didn't have electricity at the time, his uncle hooked up a washing-machine motor to a gasoline engine and used a leather-belt drive system to provide power to the lathe. This type of setup was common at the time and can still be found in some old shops, along with overhead countershafts and pulley systems.

Bob used his workshop to make reproductions inspired by pictures in books and magazines, which he sold to neighbors, and to repair furniture. When he created turnings, he generally made spindles for furniture or other commonly turned items, such as baseball bats, honey dippers, or tops. He never made bowls or other types of vessels. Though the

A close-up view of Bob's burned–in signature on the staff of the longer, ornate walking stick.

Depression made it difficult for Bob's father to get money for the crops, Bob's extra money from turning helped. The Stocksdales had no difficulty feeding the family.

Even though Bob was a completely self-taught woodworker, at age 20, his woodworking skills landed him a job in a factory for a company in Huntington called Caswell-Runyan. They built cedar chests and radio cabinets, which were made with veneers and not the solid wood that Bob preferred.

Bob's second factory job, making baker's supplies, involved using power machinery. The company specialized in large, flat ladles for taking baked goods out of ovens. Here, he graduated to making all of the implements as well as operating all of the machines in the shop. Although the products seemed simple enough, one of the plywood implements required a very fine taper, and the piece involved operations on twenty different machines. The job lasted for about two years, during which time Bob lived at home on the farm and commuted to the city to work.

In 1942, Bob followed in his older brother's footsteps and claimed conscientious objector (CO) status during World War II, a decision that did not sit well with many family members. Bob claimed CO status because he believed war did not solve anything. The Stocksdale brothers were sent to CO camps to perform alternative civilian service.

Bob's first camp, located in Valhalla, Michigan, was established on an old Civilian Conservation Corps (CCC) site. Because all of the wood had been stripped from the site to rebuild Chicago after the Great Fire, the primary job for the COs was reforesting it with white pine.

Bob approached some of the camp's leaders about his woodworking skills. The leaders agreed Bob should act as the resident

A close-up view of the simple turned knob of the plain walking stick.

woodworker and help fix some of the deteriorating buildings at the camp. They also decided to use the shop as a way to provide recreation for the COs. Because his home and tools were relatively nearby, Bob volunteered to bring his band saw and lathe for the proposed shop. His only requirement was that the tools be sent on to him when he left the camp.

It was at this first camp—and on the whimsical suggestion of one of the forestry leaders—that Bob attempted his first bowl, which was made of cherry. After that, Bob ended up making bowls and plates because of their simplicity and perhaps because of the small amount of time required to make them. As Bob was making bowls in camp, he was able to establish contact with a few wood suppliers, and he began his excellent skill of finding just the right wood for his turned projects.

Also in 1942, Bob met Helen Winnemore, owner of Helen Winnemore's Arts and Crafts in Columbus, Ohio. Because of her religious background as a Quaker, she visited the CO camps. In Valhalla, she met Bob and discovered his turned bowls. Impressed by the quality of the pieces, she offered to sell them at her gallery.

Bob worked on bowls, plates, and trays whenever he had time in camp and sent them to Helen. Through her gallery, he was able to sell all of the bowls he made. Right from the start, he signed each piece, noted the type of wood, and noted where the wood was from. Dates for the bowls were not part of Bob's signature until later in his career.

From the very beginning, Bob signed his bowls and noted the type of wood and where it was from. He did not start dating his pieces until later in his career.

About one and one-half years after Bob was assigned to the Valhalla camp, the government decided to move some of the camps out west for other work. Bob was given a choice: he could go to Oregon or California. He chose Santa Barbara. "I did some checking, and it rained a lot in Oregon, and they would make you go out in the rain. In California, it also rained, but they did not make you go out and work," Bob explains. Six months later, the COs were again moved, this time to the Feather River camp in California, east of San Francisco, where the COs provided fire suppression services. Bob's woodworking shop moved with him from camp to camp.

Bob and the other COs received 2½ days of leave time each month, plus extra leave for time spent fighting fires. Most of them found work on their time off because COs were not paid for their work, and many had to support their families. Many of the families lived right next door to the camp. Through a fellow CO, Bob began working for Hudson Antiques in Berkeley doing restoration and repair work. Today, the shop is still located just down the street from Bob's Oregon Street home. The dealer would save work for Bob, who would then complete it on his time off.

While Bob was at the Feather River camp in 1945, one of his friends and fellow COs suggested he sell his bowls to Gump's, a department store in San Francisco. When they met with Bob, Gump's buyers said they would take nearly anything Bob could make, which wasn't much because Bob had little time for his turnings. This was his first exposure to a national audience.

In 1945, Bob was released from CO camp and decided to stay in the Berkeley area. He and two friends purchased a house at 2145 Oregon Street. Because the other two men had families, Bob lived in the small room off the back of the house. From the start, Bob's primary concern was having a workshop in the basement, because turning was to be his principal means of making money. The basement had a rough dirt floor and needed some work. Fortunately, one of Bob's CO friends was a carpenter, and he was able to fix many of the problems with the basement. According to the *Oakland Tribune*, Bob's shop was 32 feet by 18 feet (9.75 meters by 5.5 meters). Throughout his life, he kept the same shop in the basement, which was often described as cave-like. Here, he kept part of a twenty-ton stock of wood.

With his own workshop completed by 1946, Bob continued selling bowls to Gump's and began selling bowls to Fraser's department store in Berkeley. Gump's sold Bob's more functional bowls, such as salad bowls and platters, while Fraser's showed Bob's decorative pieces made from exotic woods. It was through Gump's and Fraser's that Bob began to be a collected artist, with collectors such as Forrest Merrill and Bob Anderson.

GUMP'S
Exclusively in good taste

Gourmet's delight

Mahogany salad bowl of exquisite texture and shape ... a signed original, hand-crafted by Bob Stocksdale. 12 inches in diameter, it costs but 25.00 with handmade mahogany servers. In the 8½ inch size, only 18.00. Matching 8½ inch individual bowls, 4.00 each. Add 3% Sales Tax in California. Address: 250 Post St., San Francisco

GUMP'S • SAN FRANCISCO
CARMEL • HONOLULU

✳ **GIFTS**
recently advertised in
The New Yorker...
practical enough
to give yourself.

A flyer from Gump's shows mahogany salad bowls described as "Exclusively in good taste, gourmet's delight." The bowls sold for $25 and $35.

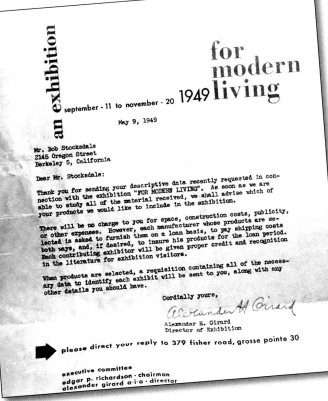

Neiman Marcus Letter Requests Selections, from Mrs. Cay Vedder, Merchandise Manager, Decorative Galleries, August 16, 1950

My dear Mr. Stocksdale:

Pardon the delay in answering your letter, but I have just returned from abroad and am beginning to catch up on accumulated correspondence. It was very nice hearing from you again and we are definitely interested in some of your things for the fall.

It so happens that Mr. Edward Marcus is vacationing in California and plans to go to San Francisco. I am forwarding a copy of this letter to him, giving him your telephone number....and I feel certain within the next week he will contact you and make some selections for us for our fall business.

An invitation to the *For Modern Living* exhibition, Detroit Institute of Arts, September 11 to November 20, 1949.

By 1950, Bob alone owned the house on Oregon Street and had married Nan Beatty. By 1951, they had started a family of their own with the birth of their first child, Joy Edith, and in 1952, they welcomed a son, Kim Charles. During that decade, Bob's career began to take off as well. He did turning demonstrations at places such as Fraser's, the Los Angeles County Fair, and the California State Fair, and he attended the American Craft Council Conference of American Craftsmen in Asilomar, California. His first solo exhibition was in 1958 at the Long Beach Museum of Art in California.

Varied Materials Available for Craftsmen,

Excerpts from the San Francisco Examiner August 17, 1952

In woodworking, the wood you use can make the difference between an ordinary product and a work of art.

Finding the right wood for whatever you are making may take time. But the results will be gratifying.

There are a multitude of unusual hardwoods particularly suitable for wooden bowls, trays and bookends....

Grain Important

When looking for wood for your shop work the first thing to look for is color and grain. Hardness is also a factor that must be taken into account. The harder the wood, the better it will withstand the rigors of turning on the lathe. Rare wood...costs more than ordinary wood. Many sell by the pound. However, by careful cutting expensive woods may be utilized without too much waste.

Rare Wood

Professional woodworker Bob Stocksdale says he spends the greatest part of his time scouring the lumber yards for rare and unusual woods.

Currently in his workshop in Berkeley, he is turning out Indian rosewood salad bowls.

Because he is in commercial operation, Stocksdale buys his lumber in large lots. Some of his pieces of rosewood weigh between 200 and 300 pounds and come in 10 feet (3 meters) lengths, 4 inches (102 millimeters) thick and 16 inches (406 millimeters) wide.

To make a 4-by-10 inch (102-by-254 millimeters) rosewood salad bowl, he first cuts out the rough circular shape from the large lumber with a band saw, cutting at a 45-degree angle. The piece is thus wider at the top than at the bottom. If the wood is slightly green, he covers the rough forms with paraffin to prevent cracking until he is ready to turn them.

For turning, he uses a standard shop lathe and gouges of various sizes. The size gouge he uses is determined by the stage of turning. Smaller gouges are used when the wood is closer to its final shape. He turns the outer surface of the bowl first. When he has turned this to the proper shape, he then reverses the bowl and turns the inside.

Bob Stocksdale at work on mahogany salad bowl.

Sharp Tools

When making small decorative bowls, Stocksdale places a piece of wood between the bowl and the lathe's faceplate to prevent the surface from being marred.

Stocksdale has turned some bowls and trays down to one-sixteenth inch (1.5 millimeters) thick. The trick for such fine turning, he says, is sharp tools. Razor sharp tools are his credo for all woodworking. If sharp tools have been used in turning, less sanding, the next step, is necessary.

The final step is the finish. On most salad bowls, Stocksdale soaks them in mineral oil. Some woods require longer soaking depending upon how much natural oil they contain. Rosewood needs to be soaked overnight while mahogany must be soaked considerably longer.

The beauty of the wood itself often determines the finish. For the majority of his rare wood decorative bowls and trays, Stocksdale uses rubbed varnish. He sprays clear floor varnish onto the freshly turned project, allows it to dry, and then rubs it by hand with pumice stone.

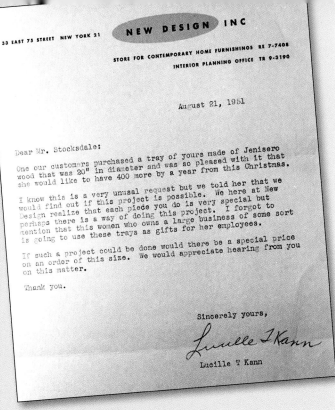

A 1951 letter requests 400 bowls as gifts for a company's employees.

New Design Inc letter:

33 EAST 75 STREET   NEW YORK 21

NEW DESIGN INC

STORE FOR CONTEMPORARY HOME FURNISHINGS   RE 7-7408
INTERIOR PLANNING OFFICE   TR 9-3190

August 21, 1951

Dear Mr. Stocksdale:

One our customers purchased a tray of yours made of Jenisero wood that was 20" in diameter and was so pleased with it that she would like to have 400 more by a year from this Christmas.

I know this is a very unusal request but we told her that we would find out if this project is possible. We here at New Design realize that each piece you do is very special but perhaps there is a way of doing this project. I forgot to mention that this women who owns a large business of some sort is going to use these trays as gifts for her employees.

If such a project could be done would there be a special price on an order of this size. We would appreciate hearing from you on this matter.

Thank you.

Sincerely yours,

Lucille T Kann

Lucille T Kann

Neiman Marcus Letter Praises Work,
from Mr. Edward Murchison, Gift Buyer, The Galleries, November 4, 1953

I am going to be perfectly honest with you, the bowls are so beautiful, and we always have them prominently displayed, but we have difficulty convincing people they should pay such prices for salad bowls. They're a strange breed here—they'll pay a fortune for a mink coat, but expect a salad bowl to cost from $5-$10. Our sales people love your bowls and play them up as much as possible and it remains that we have much more of an educational job to do. We have no difficulty getting admiration of your bowls; it's just the price we have to counteract. It certainly isn't that they aren't worth the price but convincing customers is another matter. The bowl you sent the photograph of is magnificent and I would like to order four of them if they are still available. I have been in New York for at least two weeks, hence the delay. Will you let me know?

Bob had many other exhibitions of his work throughout his life, in places such as New York City; Chicago; St. Louis; Milan, Italy; Dublin, Ireland; Japan; and many others. He also spoke at many universities and conferences in the United States and around the world. Bob's work appears in the permanent collections of renowned museums, including the Smithsonian Institution and the Metropolitan Museum of Art.

Bob's marriage to Kay Sekimachi in 1972 proved to be a significant event both personally and professionally. An artist herself, Kay began weaving in 1950. The two influenced each other's work and eventually did an exhibition together from 1993 to 1996 called "Marriage in Form" that traveled to six locations across the United States. In an interview before Bob's death, Kay said her marriage to Bob brought much more travel into her life. "We certainly go on more trips. I do quite a few workshops. I think my life changed more than his life when we got married. I did very little traveling before we were married, and suddenly I found myself really on the road because he really loves it. He's done a lot of traveling, and he'll go back to London at the drop of a hat. I think one of the first trips we took was a year after we were married. He said he thought I ought to meet his family. I had never taken a trip across the country, and so here I found myself driving across the country. My traveling days began. I always end up enjoying it."

Of course, a large part of Bob's legacy is his attention to and selection of wood. "Bob's very excited about wood," Kay said in that same interview. "He's always excited about finding new woods." She also explained how his sensitivity to wood was lacking in some of the newer woodturners: "You take a piece of wood, and there may be several ways to make a beautiful bowl out of that wood, but there aren't that many different things that you can do to it. I think the piece of wood will tell you what to do with it, to bring out the best in the piece of wood. You have to be sensitive to it, and I think that's what he has—he really does have sensitivity. I think many of these younger people are trying to go beyond that, and maybe you just can't. You don't want to ruin the integrity of the wood."

Another part of Bob's legacy is the functional elegance of his work. He brought woodturning to an art form, but he also often strove for utility and accessibility and never wanted his pieces to become simply art to push boundaries. As Kay explained, "I think a lot of people are doing things just to be different. They want to call attention to themselves, and they may do something outrageous. This is what Wendell Castle does, and he's very honest about that. He says he wants (his work) to be known as art; he's really not making furniture, he's making art, and his things are avant-garde."

Georg Jensen Shop Letter Requests Work, from Mr. W. C. Hublitz, Merchandise Manager, October 26, 1953

Dear Mr. Stocksdale,

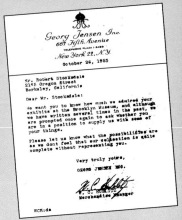

We want you to know how much we admired your exhibits at the Brooklyn Museum, and although we have written several times in the past, we are prompted to ask once again if you are in a position to supply us with some of your things.

Please let us know what the possibilities are as we don't feel that our collection is quite complete without representing you.

Questions Sent to Bob Stocksdale, from Mr. Arthur W. Baum, Associate Editor, *Saturday Evening Post*, November 9, 1953:

Dear Mr. Stocksdale:

I would appreciate it if you could write me a bit of information about your woodturning and any other handcraft activity that you practice for possible use in a handcraft article we are preparing....

What sort of regular work were you in at the time that your woodworking was a spare-time activity, and where did you live? How did you first happen to take up woodturning? What sort of shop do you operate now in Berkeley? Wasn't the laminated plywood one-ended bookend that America House used to stock a product of yours? What in the world is harewood, out of which you made the beautiful platter now at Brooklyn Museum? Is the Berkeley shop working out to your satisfaction? Are you doing any teaching?

In the article resulting from these questions in the March 13, 1954, Saturday Evening Post, *Bob described himself as a wood lathe artisan who makes pieces from forty different exotic woods and makes his sales to ten shops across the country. Outlets include America House, the Georg Jensen Shop in New York, and Gump's (author's analysis).*

Woodturner Returns to His Roots, 1953

Excerpts from the Huntington Indiana Herald-Press:
Bob Stocksdale with his mother, Mrs. R.C. Stocksdale, looking at decorative and serviceable bowls and platters. Visiting with his two children Joy Edith & Kim. His parents lived on Union Center Road. Bob Stocksdale began woodworking while still a student at Union Township High School, making several intricately hand-carved pieces of furniture. He discovered California black walnut and Oregon myrtle wood because they had much more interesting grain. Stocksdale also has with him pieces made of magnolia, grey harewood from England, zebrawood from Africa, amaranth from British Guiana, mahogany from Guatemala, and koa from Hawaii. Stocksdale no longer wholesales his work. House Beautiful magazine has asked for an interview. He is reputed to be the only person in the country who makes thin bowls—as slim as 3/32" (2.4mm)—with a satin smooth finish and for the beauty and uniqueness of the type of wood.

A 1955 letter from Senator Richard Neuberger.

RICHARD L. NEUBERGER
OREGON

JOHN G. JONES
ADMINISTRATIVE ASSISTANT
MARY JANE CHRISTGAU
PERSONAL SECRETARY

United States Senate
WASHINGTON, D. C.

February 16, 1955

Mr. Robert Stockdale
2145 Oregon Street
Berkeley 5, California

Dear Mr. Stockdale:

I have learned through Mr. Ursell, who has that admirable modern furnishings shop in Georgetown, of your kind remarks about me.

I am glad to learn that you share my point of view on many issues. My wife and I certainly admire your beautiful wooden bowls.

I hope you will call at my office if you ever come to Washington.

Sincerely,

Richard L. Neuberger

RLN:hn

"Maybe the ACC (American Crafts Council) had something to do with it, too. With the exposure of *Craft Horizons* (magazine, now *American Craft* magazine) and America House, a craft showroom in Manhattan during the *Craft Horizons* era, more and more people began to take crafts seriously."

Because of his role in elevating woodturning to an art form, "Bob is now a member of the woodworking establishment and is looked to as a role model. He is a consummate woodturner," Kay noted. Though he was known to tell visiting craftsmen they could "come as long as you don't stay too long," Bob did inspire many woodturners. However, he never formally gave instruction, except for an occasional demonstration.

In addition to being known for his turning excellence and his gift for finding the best wood, Bob had a wonderful work ethic and managed to balance his work and his personal life well. As Kay explained, "Bob is very disciplined. He's there at 9 a.m. and out by 3:30 p.m. and never works on the weekends. That's the way it has been."

9

Bonniers Letter Requests Bowls,
from Mr. Goran Holmquist, January 21, 1957

Dear Mr. Stockdale:

I was very glad to meet you and to see the fine work you are doing in wood.

This is to remind you that I will be interested in receiving three of the very big walnut bowls, 18 inches (457mm) in diameter and 7 inches (176mm) high. You indicated the price to be about $40 each. And also I would like twenty-four of the individual salad bowls like the sample you showed me. The price for these, you told me, was $2.50 each.

There is no great rush but if I could have them sometime in April, it would be very good.

Finding Cocobolo, November 27, 1960

Excerpts from an article in **Bonanza**, *a Bay Area newspaper:*
One of Stocksdale's best finds was at Playland at the beach where he came upon some unusual cocobolo wood that had been imported from Central America more than twenty years ago. The wood was hard enough to make bearings for the ride equipment and could be cut with woodworking tools. When Playland officials began farming out the making of the bearings, a cache of fourteen logs was left over. Stocksdale picked them up in a storage yard where they had been exposed to the weather. He also got some jussaro wood that had been set aside in a San Francisco store fixture shop because someone had complained the dust from the wood acted the same as sneezing powder. Stocksdale opens all windows and works it without sneezing.

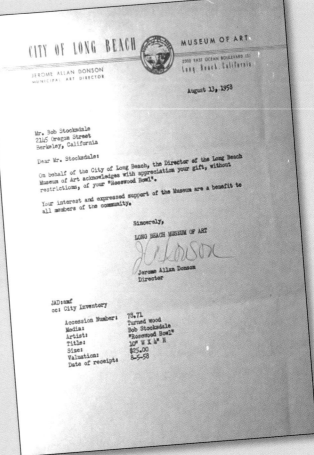

Bob donated a rosewood bowl to the Long Beach Museum of Art after his first solo exhibition, held there in 1958. This letter thanks him for the donation.

Stocksdale on Choosing Wood,
Excerpts from the Christian Science Monitor, June 22, 1961

"When I take up a piece of wood and begin to work with it, one of the main ideas I have in my mind is to try and bring out all of its natural beauty." As Mr. Stocksdale puts it: "I had never thought about turning bowls, but because I didn't have a lot of raw materials in the camp, I was able to get a few pieces of hardwood. I tried turning a few pieces of wood on the lathe and started making bowls. I don't have a design in mind when I start. The first thing I do with a piece of wood is to get as large a circle as possible out of the block. I band saw it out and then I put it on the lathe and turn off any flaws that show, like bark or a knot or sapwood that I don't like. Then I design the bowl, if the design hasn't already evolved from the elimination of the flaws. Quite often, I'll work out a new shape by just eliminating flaws. But of course, all wood doesn't have flaws. I always turn the outside of the bowl first and design the shape of the bowl from the outside and then just make the inside contour just the same as the outside. You usually get a lot more out of a piece of wood than you expect.

"Many of the qualities in a piece of wood are developed by the way a piece is finished. My pieces are as near as the natural color of the wood as possible. I never stain or dye any of the wood. For that reason, I have to choose my wood. Not only the type of wood but the particular pieces. I'll go through a whole pile of timber and just pick out one or two pieces. One can use five or six different finishes on the type of work I do. These depend on the color of the wood, the hardness of it, and the purpose for which the piece is going to be used. Generally, you just can't leave a piece of wood raw when it comes off the lathe. However there are exceptionally hard woods like South American cocobolo and Lignum Vitae that require no oil or varnish or other finish and are complete after sanding with a polishing from its own shavings. Walnut, for instance, to be used for a salad bowl gets a different finish than if it is going to be used for a tray. All the salad bowl needs is a soaking in mineral oil. I just let it soak for two or three days and then the bowl can be washed and the oil can come back out to the surface again. But the same walnut used for a tray has to be treated differently, because a tray will quite often have glasses sit on it that are wet and they can leave rings. So, I have to put on a varnish that is not so much affected by moisture. When it has dried, I rub it with pumice stone and oil. I am always on the lookout for a new and interesting wood but my favorite wood is the California black walnut because it has so many variations in color and texture."

In answer to a question about how he makes his showpieces: "Quite often, I don't realize I have a showpiece until it is entirely finished. I try to make each piece I make into a showpiece, of course it doesn't always work out that way, but that is what I try to do." Museums that have exhibited Stocksdale's work include: the San Francisco Museum of Art, the Smithsonian Institution, the Museum of Modern Art, Buffalo Fine Arts Academy, the Cleveland Museum of Art, the City Art Museum in St. Louis, and the Minneapolis Institute of Arts. Two of Stocksdale's bowls were placed in the American exhibit at the 1958 World's Fair held in Brussels. One was a California black walnut salad bowl and the other was a cocobolo decorative bowl that was turned down to one-thirty-secondth of an inch (.8 millimeters)—so thin it was translucent.

DINNER IN HONOR

OF

HIS EXCELLENCY URHO KEKKONEN

PRESIDENT OF FINLAND

Sponsored by

THE FINNISH-AMERICAN SOCIETIES

IN NORTHERN CALIFORNIA

OCTOBER 27, 1961

FAIRMONT HOTEL · SAN FRANCISCO

An invitation to dinner, on October 27, 1961, in honor of the President of Finland, Urho Kekkonen, for whom Bob designed a swirling-grain redwood burl tray.

Bob at work at the lathe in 1968.

Bob married Kay Sekimachi, a fiber artist, in 1972. For the *Marriage in Form* exhibition that they did together in 1993, Kay made paper vessels using Bob's bowls as forms.

Bob was always involved with a variety of groups, such as the California Crafts Guild, the Baulines Craft Guild, and the International Wood Collectors Society, as well as with individual craftsmen, including Sam Maloof. As Bob's fame grew, so did demands on him to attend shows and inquiries from galleries. Both Kay and Bob found the requests a little overwhelming. "I think that more galleries would like to have his work," said Kay. "He gets inquiries all the time, but we just don't need that anymore. The same is true with me. He sells direct—less work and more money.

"I know I get very irritated because I accept an invitation to a show, and then it comes time to ship. I get irritated because I have to pack and ship it. The shows have increased. The Bay Area, or maybe California in general, has increased in the support of the crafts; there is more happening. In this area, you could practically go to an opening every night. There's the California Crafts Gallery and the San Francisco Museum of Craft and Folk Art, which is another one we try to support, one that is trying to be a real museum and show old and contemporary. In weaving, we have the Pacific Basin School of Textile Arts, we've got Fiberworks, plus California College of Arts and Crafts (now California College of the Arts)." (Text continues on page 18.)

Woodcrafting, Bay Area Style

San Francisco Chronicle, Thursday, December 21, 1978, by Barbara Falconer Newhall

On the floor of Bob Stocksdale's garage in Berkeley stands a knee-high, weather-beaten partially rotted log. One more stroke of the ax and this piece of wood would fit nicely into the fireplace. Or so it seems to the unpracticed eye.

When Stocksdale looks at the log, he sees bowls, two large ones, perhaps, or several small ones. When a fellow woodworker—who offered Stocksdale $200 for the log—looked at it, he saw a violin.

The log is Brazilian rosewood, which is very difficult to come by these days. And Stocksdale, who in a matter of hours can turn a lesser piece of wood into a delicate, feather-light bowl or plate that will fetch as much as $100, is not willing to part with this particular piece of rosewood.

Not that Stocksdale, a newly appointed Fellow of the American Crafts Council, is short on logs. He has been plying his craft—technically known as woodturning—for thirty-five years, and he has been collecting wood for decades. Filling the garage, the basement and the yard of the house he has lived in since he moved to Berkeley after World War II, are hardwood logs of every sort.

African muninga, Oregon yew, Madagascar rosewood, African blackwood (the hardest wood of all to work), pernambuco, Arizona desert ironwood, some black walnut from Los Gatos, teak from Thailand (also becoming scarce), pieces of rosewood from India purchased in London, black acacia from a tree felled recently on the Mills College campus and the remnants of a log of zebrawood bought in New York fifteen years ago. In short, there lies aging in Stockdale's backyard thousands of dollars worth of wood.

Some people look at a block of wood and see a block of wood. Berkeley area woodturner Bob Stocksdale instead sees a bowl, a plate, or a violin.

Editor's Note: The story that appears here is from the Chronicle. The images that appeared with that story were not available for publication, so others have been substituted.

15

Much of it was given to him by admirers. "I never turn down anything," said Stocksdale. If nothing else, he and his wife, weaver Kay Sekimachi, "have two fireplaces."

A piece of wood that is destined to be a salad bowl or a collector's item, however, is cut into a crosswise piece about the width of the bowls it is to become and then cut into blanks with a band saw. The blanks are roughed into bowls with a lathe, chuck, and turning tools.

If the wood is still moist, the roughed-out bowls go into the drying room, where they remain for two to four weeks, until the bowl is ready for finishing on the lathe. Most wood turners won't begin work on a piece of wood at all until the entire section of log is dry; Stocksdale speeds up the drying process by cutting the log down into roughed out bowls before drying. If the piece is to be a salad bowl, a mineral oil finish is all that is needed. Otherwise, Stocksdale might use bar top lacquer.

Stocksdale, who was born in Indiana, became an expert with the lathe during his 3½ year stint in conscientious objector camps during World War II.

Between fighting fires and repairing equipment at a CO camp at Feather River, the young Stocksdale found time to work at the lathe, turning out bowls that found a ready market at no less prestigious an outlet than Gump's in San Francisco.

Berkeley's Bob Stocksdale: Local Wood Turner Gains National Fame,

by Gordon Raddue, Excerpts from the Independent and Gazette, January 27, 1979

Berkeley—Local wood turner Bob Stocksdale doesn't let a lack of competition lull him in his quest for artistic perfection.

His success at fashioning logs and planks into artistic masterpieces by means of a lathe have earned him the highest honor the nation can bestow on a craftsman.

When he was named one of ten artists to receive an American Craft Council Fellow award for 1978, he became one of only forty-six people so honored since the inception of the award four years ago.

Stocksdale, who collected the award in ceremonies held at the Museum of Contemporary Crafts in New York City, believes he may be the last woodturner to reap the honor.

"One of the prerequisites for winning the award is you have to be in the crafts field for at least twenty years, and not many woodturners stick with it that long," he said. "I don't have any competition in all of the United States."

Stocksdale isn't the only distinguished craftsperson at his Oregon Street home. His wife is the famous weaver, Kay Sekimachi. Both will soon be exhibiting their work in New York City.

Stocksdale's daughter, Joy, is gifted at stitchery and quilting. She is presently a student at the University of London's crafts school, Goldsmith College.

"It's quite an honor just to be accepted at Goldsmith," her father noted.

Since finding correctly seasoned wood is an important part of his craft, Stocksdale imports much of his material from distant parts of the world, though he also works with California black walnut.

Most of his wood comes from England and France.

"London is a better source of supply than any place in this country," he said. "It gets wood from former colonies all over the world."

Both Stocksdale and his wife enjoy international reputations. Both are represented in the permanent collections in the Oakland Museum and other museums. They are also represented in many private collections, including the Johnson Company's "Objects: USA."

Stocksdale's numerous honors include a citation from the U.S. Department of State for his participation in the 1958 Brussels exhibition. He specializes in masterly crafted, personally designed bowls and serving trays. He has fashioned bowls with a wall so thin that light shines through.

The only local outlet for his products is the Arts and Crafts Cooperative Inc., 1652 Shattuck Avenue. However, he sells a great deal of them at various shows around the country; he sold ten of the fourteen pieces he exhibited in Philadelphia last year for a total in excess of $1,100.

The most money he has ever received for a single piece was $500 for an ebony bowl.

While his wife combines two days a week of teaching at Fort Mason in San Francisco with her art work, Stocksdale has never been involved in instruction, except for an occasional demonstration. His latest demonstration was at Dartmouth College in New Hampshire while he was back East to receive his American Craft Council Fellowship.

He was the only Californian among the ten artists cited for 1978.

In announcing the award, the council extolled Stocksdale as "an exemplary artist who has set a standard by his own work."

Bob Stocksdale displays some of his vessels.

Origins of the Paper Bowls, Shown at 'Marriage in Form'

Excerpts from an interview with Kay Sekimachi,
Bob Stocksdale's wife conducted by the author in 1987

Bob's daily output was steady and meant bowls could be found everywhere in the house. He usually brought roughed-out bowls to the kitchen to sit on cabinet tops and dry before turning them to their final form. There were bowls drying in the downstairs finishing room and choice pieces displayed on tables throughout the house. So it was only natural that Kay would at some point turn to rough-turned bowl forms to mold her paper bowls on and to produce what has been recognized as Bob and Kay's most successful collaboration. The following are Kay's reminiscences of how it all happened:

"Weaving is the slowest process....One morning, I was laying in bed thinking it would be nice if I did something more direct, something that went much more quickly. I just happened to start thinking about all my linen thrums—the leftover warp ends. Linen is so beautiful that I save the ends. So I had this bag of thrums, I also had this material called Stitch Witchery....It puts glue on both surfaces. You can lay two pieces together and fuse them with a steam iron. I thought, 'Why can't I throw a few threads around a ceramic bowl, lay some stitch witchery, and lay my steam iron on it?' So, I got up and got to work. I think I get all of my best ideas when I am relaxing, mulling things over in my mind. The thread design turned out to be very much like a bird's nest, very light and airy...."

Flax Bowl, 1987, 4" x 8¾" (102mm x 222mm), unspun flax, paper, silver, gold, gel medium, and matte lacquer. *(Photo by Charles Frizzell.)*

"Then, I started playing around with laminating linen fragments, placing lace samplers in between two pieces of rice paper, and pounding. I was just experimenting with different approaches, and some of them turned out looking like potshards. This potshard effect was flat; it wasn't on a form yet....Then, I guess the idea came to me to try a paper bowl wrapped around one of Bob's forms. I already had rice paper for doing a series of woven books....The first step in coloring the materials would be to paint the image with dyes on a piece of transfer paper....Then, I make my warp and stretch the warp across the ironing board. I then lay layers of paper to take the dyed image and press it onto the warp threads....I found that the image that I got on the piece of paper was very interesting because of all of the lines going through it.

"I think that one of the first paper bowls I made was around a pot that a friend made. I used all white rice paper, and took my linen threads and put them all around. The paper had to have the paste already on it; then I just went around and around, quickly cut pieces of paper, and put it on top. So actually, it's just linen threads laminated between. It looked coiled and very much like paper lanterns....That's how I started this business with what I call bird nest baskets—linen threads fused together....

"I was surprised when they were well received. At one point, I was selling one a month. I still don't think of these as my serious work....It's more spontaneous. In that sense, it's more like pottery. I could do this with visitors.... Anyway, it just sort of fits into my life now. And it's fun, experimental, and spontaneous. You're never sure how it's going to turn out....

"Is there any precedent for this type of artwork? I've not seen any, although my friend, Sylvia Seventy, does them with brown paper bags. Hers are very different from mine, because I really like translucency and the overlapping of transparent planes. I like to see what happens when you overlap two pieces of paper or cloth. When I started, my friends came over, and all of sudden, I started getting all kinds of paper from everybody. I got handmade silk paper, handmade indigo-dyed paper. June Schwarcz gave me her whole collection of handmade rice paper, and so I suddenly feel I'm obligated to continue on with this...."

(Continued from page 13.)
"Maybe the ACC helped to legitimize the crafts. More exhibitions, street fairs, state fairs, art festivals, and it kept growing out of the 1950s and the 1960s....That's how a lot of people started—by exhibiting at the state fairs."

Bob garnered several awards in his lifetime. Both Bob and Kay were inducted as Fellows of the American Craft Council. Bob received his ACC Fellowship in 1978 as "an exemplary artist who has set a standard by his own work," according to the *Independent and Gazette*. He was also honored as a California Living Treasure and as an Honorary Lifetime Member of the American Association of Woodturners and was awarded a gold medal from the ACC and the first Lifetime Achievement Award from the Collectors of Wood Art.

Bob also seems to have passed along his love and talent for handcrafts to his daughter, Joy. She is a gifted quilter and attended the University of London's craft school, Goldsmith College.

Bob Stocksdale's life as a craftsman seems to have been hard-coded in his DNA. True, there certainly was enough serendipity and encouragement along the way to set the conditions for him to explore and discover his talents, but without the combination of inner resourcefulness, persistence, and a natural affinity for the medium, he would never have thrived.

Bob's salad bowls are wonderful examples of form and function combined. This set is made of pistachio wood.

Though Bob never gave formal instruction, he did several demonstrations during his career. Often, Bob would create an impressive layered pile of shavings during his demonstrations.

Kay on Bob and the Growth of Woodworking versus the Growth of Weaving
Excerpts from an interview with Kay Sekimachi on Crafts and Their Place in Society conducted by the author in 1987

For many years, Bob was a local crafts hero. But in the 1970s and 1980s, he seemed to become more widely known. It's the time. Woodworking has sort of come into it's own. Weaving, I think, peaked much before the 1970s. People were weaving all over the country....
I started in 1950, and at that time, the only people who were weaving were fairly well-to-do ladies who had the time to weave, who had the money to buy a loom....I'm sure Haystack school was started then in weaving....In the 1960s, it was very popular, and by the 1970s, it was no longer just weaving on the loom, but every kind of textile technique....

There are people who are doing serious textile research; they go and work with a Navajo weaver and write books about it. It's also happening in Japan. There's even a group of weavers called the Complex Weavers Guild, and they study the more complex weave structures.

A 1984 paper bowl by Kay Sekimachi.

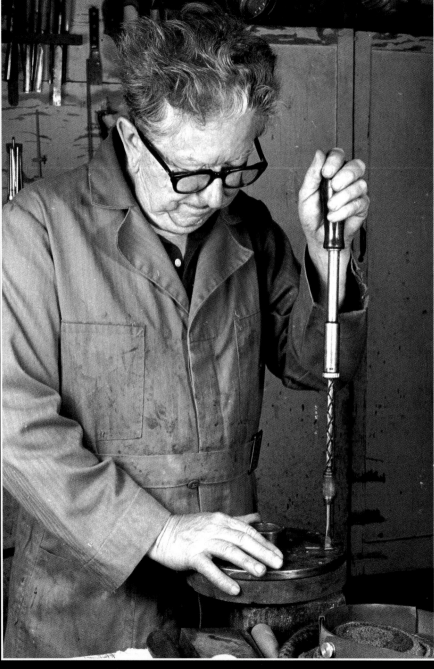

Bob mounts a faceplate onto a wooden lathe chuck.

Gallery:
A Selection of Bob Stocksdale's Work

For many of us, a daily encounter with a salad bowl is unremarkable. They are usually heavy, utilitarian pieces of common ware. Age may show in knife marks and an oil-soaked surface that, over the years, has darkened the light areas of the wood grain. In contrast, fine-art bowls are not intended to hold anything and, in fact, usually fail miserably when loaded up with fruits or nuts.

Handling one of Bob's bowls for the first time, you notice their amazing lightness. The sensation is like holding an empty eggshell. It seems to defy gravity and float above your hands. It's at this point that the encounter changes. The bowl has transcended being a container. You are no longer looking at a handmade container—you are discovering a fragile work of art.

The next sensation occurs when you feel the thickness of the walls of the bowl. Bob's bowls fall into the one-eighth to three-sixteenths inch (3.2 to 4.8 millimeter) thickness, and as you run your fingers caliper-like up and down the bowl sides, you realize the thickness is consistent, top to bottom. What you may not realize is the consistency is important to the integrity of the shape. If the bowl is too thick or too thin in sections, it will distort in shape over the years, through expansion and contraction because of changes in humidity.

Depending on the lighting in the room, you may next notice areas of translucence. The two end-grain sides glow cream or golden red from the light. Not all bowls are like this, but with those that are, the translucence creates a 3-D view of the tree's core.

The next discovery is the silhouette. Bob's approach to turning was to make the outside of the bowl first. The silhouette usually has an even sweep from lip to integrated pedestal or flat bottom. This broad sweep seems to work well with the grain of the wood. Indeed, Bob's ability to display the grain through the shape of the bowl was one of his special skills, acquired through years of working with exotic woods.

On some of Bob's bowls, the top lip is straight; on some, it is wavy to match the grain or sapwood pattern; and on others, it is natural and irregular to show off a burl pattern. As you rotate the object in our hands, you realize that while serendipity may have occurred during the process of making it, the precious art object you are holding is the result of many small decisions in a process in which Bob tied together the silhouette, the grain, and the interior into a celebration of wood.

Macadamia, Hawaii,
3¼" x 4¼" (82mm x 108mm).

Lignum Vitae, Nicaragua,
3½" x 4½" (86mm x 112mm).

Unless otherwise noted, all photos by Ron Roszkiewicz. All bowls
by Bob Stocksdale. Material, creation date, dimensions, and
current owner included when available.

To Turn the Perfect Wooden Bowl: The Lifelong Quest of Bob Stocksdale

Wild persimmon, Texas,
4¼" x 5¼" (108mm x 133mm).

Snakewood, Surinam,
4¾" x 7½" (120mm x 191mm).

Walnut.

To Turn the Perfect Wooden Bowl: The Lifelong Quest of Bob Stocksdale

Blackwood.

Magnolia.

Chapter Two **Gallery:** A Selection of Bob Stocksdale's Work

Ebony.

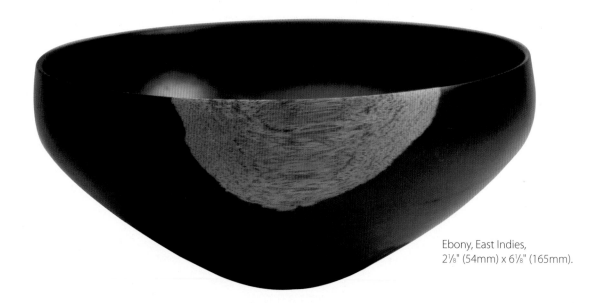

Ebony, East Indies,
2⅛" (54mm) x 6⅛" (165mm).

To Turn the Perfect Wooden Bowl: The Lifelong Quest of Bob Stocksdale

Macassar Ebony.

Pink ivory, Zululand,
3¾" x 6¼" (95mm x 158mm).

Mahogany, Honduras,
¾" x 20½" (19mm x 521mm).

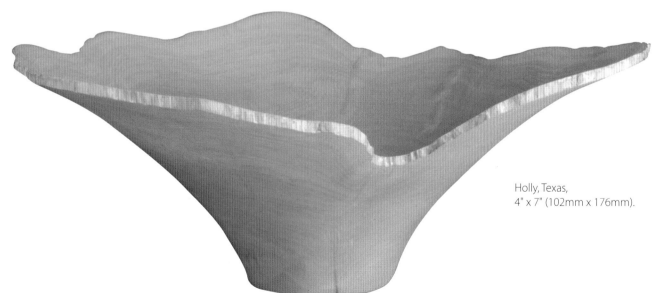

Holly, Texas,
4" x 7" (102mm x 176mm).

Pink ivory, Zululand,
3¾" (95mm) x 6¼" (158mm)

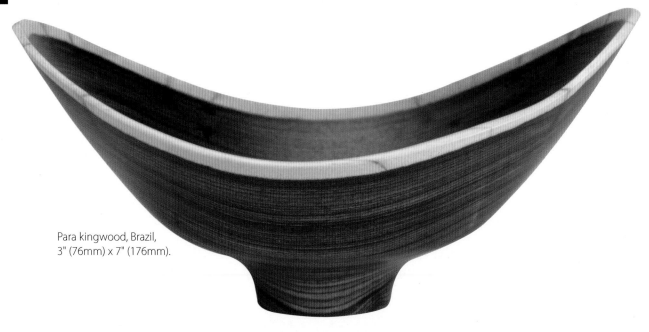

Para kingwood, Brazil,
3" (76mm) x 7" (176mm).

To Turn the Perfect Wooden Bowl: The Lifelong Quest of Bob Stocksdale

African blackwood,
4¼" x 6⅛" (108mm x 155mm).

Ebony, Malaysia,
2¾" x 6¼" (70mm x 18mm).
Collection of Sylvia and Eric Elsesser.

Ash, England,
3" x 8½" (76mm x 216mm).

Para kingwood, Brazil,
3¼" x 7⅛" (82mm x 181mm).

34

Marriage Sets from left to right: Kay Sekimachi,
"Hornet's Nest Paper Bowl," 1999,
4¼" x 7" (108mm x 176mm),
hornet's-nest paper, laminated, and Krylon coated.

Paired with Bob Stocksdale, Chichem, Mexico, 1999,
4¼" x 7" (108mm x 176mm).
Collection of Forrest L. Merrill.

Miniature Marriage in Form Set, Kay Sekimachi,
"Hornet's Nest Paper Bowl," 1993,
2¼" x 2⅝" x 2½" (57mm x 67mm x 64mm).

Paired with Bob Stocksdale, African blackwood, 1993,
2¼" x 2⅝" x 2½" (57mm x 67mm x 64mm).
Collection of Signe Mayfield.

Bob Stocksdale, Cocobolo, Guatemala, 1999,
1" x 5" x 4" (25mm x 127mm x 102mm) .

Paired with Kay Sekimachi, *Orange Paper Bowl*, 1998,
4½" x 5½" x 4½" (112mm x 140mm x 112mm),
orange antique Japanese paper, laminated, and
Krylon coated. *Collection of Paul Stricklin.*

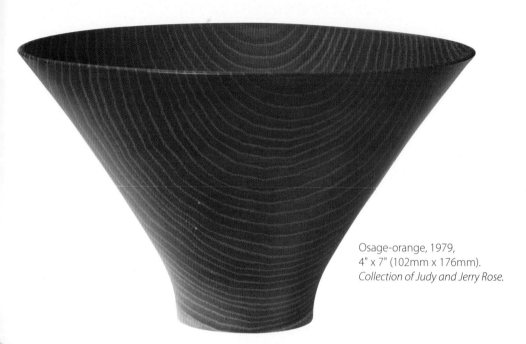

Osage-orange, 1979,
4" x 7" (102mm x 176mm).
Collection of Judy and Jerry Rose.

Smoke tree, Indiana, 1991,
3⅛" x 4¼" (79mm x 108mm).
Collection of Kay Sekimachi.

Wild persimmon, Texas,
4¼" x 5¼" (108mm x 133mm).

38

Amboyna, Malaysia, 1999,
3½" x 8¼" (86mm x 209mm).
Collection of Forrest L. Merrill.

Ebony, Malaysia, 1991,
6 ³⁄₈" x 6¼" (162mm x 158mm).
Collection of Dorothy and George Saxe.

Wild persimmon, Texas,
4¼" x 5¼" (108mm x 133mm).

Macadamia, Hawaii,
3¼" x 4¼" (82mm x 108mm).

Mesquite, Texas. 1982.
3" x 7" (76mm x 176mm).
From the Sam Maloof Collection.

To Turn the Perfect Wooden Bowl: The Lifelong Quest of Bob Stocksdale

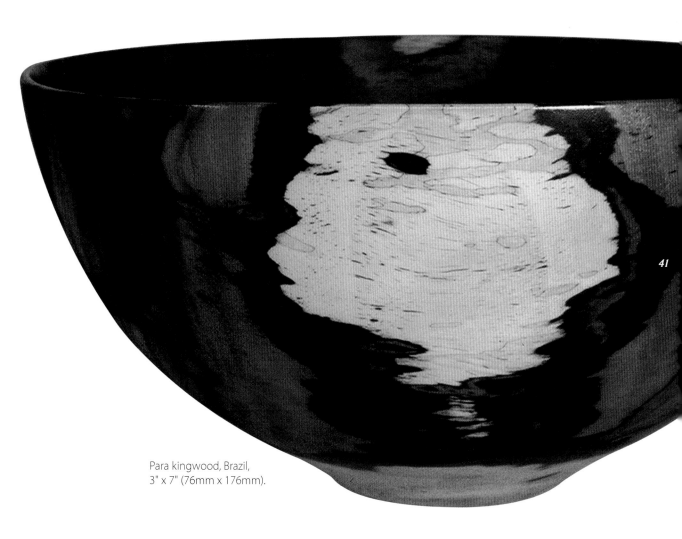

Para kingwood, Brazil,
3" x 7" (76mm x 176mm).

Walnut Salad Bowl with Paddles, 1998,
6" x 15" (152mm x 381mm).

Eucalyptus, California, 1982,
7" x 5½" (176mm x 140mm).
From the Sam Maloof Collection.

To Turn the Perfect Wooden Bowl: The Lifelong Quest of Bob Stocksdale

Large bowl, Australian blackwood,
8" x 25" (203mm x 635mm);

Small bowl, Kingwood (Violetwood),
2¾" x 6¾" (70mm x 171mm).
Photo by Stone and Steccati.

Flowering persimmon,
California, 1990,
3" (76mm) x 6" (152mm).
*From the Jerry Glaser
Collection.*

Lignum Vitae, Nicaragua,
4" x 5¾" (102mm x 146mm).
From the Sam Maloof Collection.

To Turn the Perfect Wooden Bowl: The Lifelong Quest of Bob Stocksdale

Koa, Hawaii, 1982,
4" x 4¾" (102mm x 120mm).
From the Sam Maloof Collection.

Maple, California, 1979,
3⅜" x 6⅜""
(92mm x 162mm).
From the Sam Maloof Collection.

46

Manitoba maple burl, Manitoba, 1981.
The bowl bottom shows the wood
identification and Bob's signature.
From the Jerry Glaser Collection.

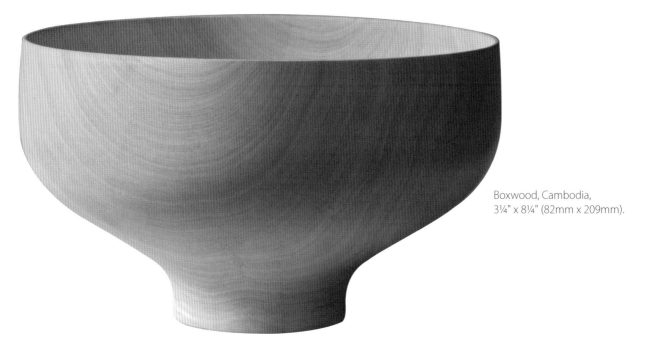

Boxwood, Cambodia,
3¼" x 8¼" (82mm x 209mm).

Ebony, Ceylon,
3½" (86mm) x 7" (176mm).
From the Jerry Glaser Collection.

Ebony, Ceylon,
3⅝" x 6⅞" (92mm x 175mm).
From the Sam Maloof Collection.

Lacewood, Australia, 1993,
2" x 8½" (51mm x 216mm).
From the Sam Maloof Collection.

To Turn the Perfect Wooden Bowl: The Lifelong Quest of Bob Stocksdale

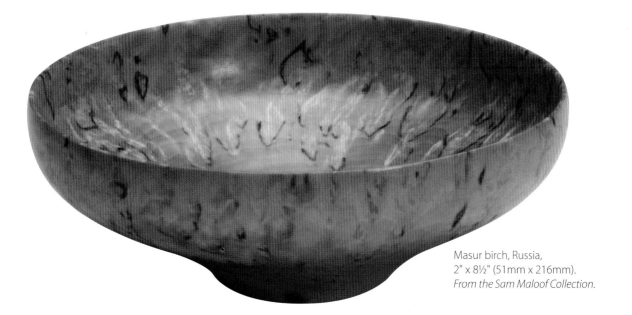

Masur birch, Russia,
2" x 8½" (51mm x 216mm).
From the Sam Maloof Collection.

Lemon, California, 1982,
5" x 6" (127mm x 152mm).
From the Sam Maloof Collection.

Partridgewood, England, 1987,
4½" x 6¾" (112mm x 171mm).
From the Sam Maloof Collection.

Macadamia, California, 1979,
4" x 6¼" (102mm x 158mm).
From the Sam Maloof Collection.

Lignum Vitae, Nicaragua,
3¼" x 9" (82mm x 229mm).
From the Sam Maloof Collection.

Bob steers a big slab of wood through his band saw to cut a disk.

Wood:
More Than a Medium

Bob Stocksdale had a nose for exotic wood and a network to help him find it. Many of the logs he collected and converted to art had heroic stories behind their discovery and delivery out of some impossible forest or mountainside. It was part of the personal connection collectors had with Bob and the pieces they acquired from him. Special logs also made their way to him through lumber merchants. Even though he was known for his work ethic and daily routine, he was always ready to hop in his truck at a moment's notice to check out a log at a boatbuilder's shop or a merchant's shed.

Bob's stock of timber was stacked under the rear deck of the house.

Q. Do you keep wood anywhere other than in your garage?

The garage has most of the wood. If I get a call from a timber supplier like Penberthy, I usually go down after it in the truck. It gives me an excuse to go to Los Angeles. I don't ever have any logs sawn by them. I may cut them in two to facilitate loading, like I did that big African blackwood log I brought up. It was just too big for four or five people to load, so we just whacked it in two with the chain saw. So, I have two pieces in the garage; one of them I've been working off. I either put them in the garage or in the basement here. I don't like to put them in the garage, especially in the summertime because the garage gets too hot. So, I put them in the basement area here. Pink ivory log, I can see it from here (in the basement). That's a good place because it also supports that piece of plywood there.

A view of the rear suburban garden at Bob's Berkeley, California, home shows it as an extension of the comfortable surroundings Bob and his wife, Kay, developed at their home over the years.

Bob's finishing room had bowls in various stages of drying or finishing.

Q. How do you decide what wood you will use?

I'll select a wood I want to work on, and I'll at least rough out a number of (bowl blanks) from a cross section and then maybe finish up completely one or two bowls from that. The rest of them I'll leave just roughed out either in that room or above the stove.

Q. Give me an idea what a typical day is in the shop, if that is possible.

One of the first things I want to do either this week or next week is to rough out some pistachio. I just got those two logs out there. I know the wood is quite fragile. It has the tendency to crack pretty badly, especially in the log, so I want to take a cross section off one of those and rough out two or three bowls, and then I'll know the condition of the rest of the log. And if I see it is doing some internal cracking or something like that, why, I'll go ahead and rough out all of the pieces out of that particular log. They're not all that big, you

see, so I can only get six or eight bowls out of each little log there, and also, I might even use polyglycol on (the sawn bowl blanks).
The last two bowls I made from a section of a log I got from Del Stubbs. I used polyglycol, and I had good success. And there's a possibility I'll rough out one and not use polyglycol on it, and use it on the others that I rough out. I'll see whether the one dries out without cracking. Look over here. That piece was 22 inches (559 millimeters) long when I got it. I found that it was all honeycombed throughout, and all I could get was a little 2-by-6-inch (51-by-152 millimeter) piece.

That roughing out will probably take me half a day or more, and then I have a little repair work on a piece that was sent back to me the other day. I'll just look around and see what I want to do. I don't have any special things planned. I do have to pack up eight bowls for two different shows. I have to keep that in mind. Because this piece of wood is sitting in my shop now, I might put it on the lathe and see if I can get a bowl out of it.

To Turn the Perfect Wooden Bowl: The Lifelong Quest of Bob Stocksdale

Q. When do you go upstairs and dip into the group of blanks over the stove?

Bob's answer below begins to address the question but veers off to something he wanted to mention. The truth is he marked roughed-out bowls and returned to them to check their progress as they reached some equilibrium with the local humidity. Because most of Bob's wood arrived in log form, he was continually dealing with moisture and ways to extract it at its own pace. For some woods, that meant storage for a time over the kitchen stove; for others, it meant coating the ends with waxy polyethylene glycol, or polyglycol.

Thirty years ago, I couldn't get that good a quality of wood. I didn't have the sources yet. Then, I got a contact in Houston. The sources developed in the last twenty years or so. But thirty years ago, I had a good connection in Los Angeles with a place called Tropical Hardwoods. They had a fabulous collection of rare and exotic woods. As a matter of fact, you'd go there, and if you wanted the middle of that timber there, they'd just cut it up for you. It never bothered them in the least to cut up a section, a circle, or anything like that out of a plank. They would import the stuff; I never knew exactly how they got it. One of the guys had lived in the tropics and had connections, especially in Central America. They used to charge exorbitant prices for their wood. But I got acquainted with them enough, and they used to knock the prices way down for me. I didn't buy a whole lot. I'd take them the bowl to show them what I made with it, and they liked that.

Q. There was a brochure that I saw from Stemm....

Yes, Chester B. Stemm. They stripped trimmings from their veneer logs, either ends of the logs or sides, in order to get down to the good veneer to mount it on their veneer machines. They'd usually send me a half-round slab of Brazilian rosewood. In fact, I still have a couple of pieces left over from that. Then, I would make up a bunch of bowls and send them back to them, and I'd charge them for my labor—not nearly what the bowls were worth. I would also keep some of the wood for myself. They specialized in architectural veneers. If an architect specified their veneers for a job, they would get a bowl. I sent them 75 or 100 bowls altogether. Real beauties some of them, I have pictures of them.

Q. I couldn't believe you were wholesaling bowls to them at a very low price for this premium quality wood. I suppose one of the benefits of the relationship was that you were getting wood that ordinarily would not have been available to you otherwise.

Right. It was such good quality, it was veneer-quality wood.

Q. So you were able to get quality wood from Stemm, Tropical?

And Penberthy Lumber in Los Angeles. They were the biggest hardwood dealer on the West Coast. I became well acquainted with the older Mr. Penberthy. I sold him a few bowls. They were always bringing in some exotic stuff in good quantity. That Nigerian ebony they

brought in…they had 75 or 100 tons of it on one shipment. Take boxwood, for instance. They brought in the first boxwood from Cambodia. And old man Penberthy…every year he would take a trip around the world buying wood, and he ran across this boxwood in Cambodia, and when he brought it in, nobody wanted the stuff because they had never worked with it or anything. They gave him a bad time in the office for bringing it in—his sons especially. And he was complaining to me a bit, and I said, 'I'll take a couple of logs.' He sent me a couple of logs. I went out and looked at it first. They weren't big logs, 7 or 8 feet long (2.1 or 2.4 meters) and so big around. He charged me $17.50 a log. I don't know whether that was the going price or not. I have bought boxwood logs from him since. In fact, I've got one out here that I've never cut into, and that was $1 a pound, which is still very reasonable because boxwood is not all that heavy, so it only cost $35 to $40.

Boxwood, Cambodia, 3¼" x 8¼" (82mm x 209mm). This is an example of a bowl from the first boxwood imported by Penberthy into the United States.

To Turn the Perfect Wooden Bowl: The Lifelong Quest of Bob Stocksdale

Q. What about curly maple or claro walnut or burlwood?

Well, I've always used claro walnut. I've never used curly maple or bird's-eye maple. I bought a huge zebrawood log from Monteith (an exotic wood specialist based in Brooklyn). I was there in New York, and I went out to see Doug Dayton. And I asked him if he had any zebrawood, and he said he had, down in the mill in New Jersey....And he said the price was eleven cents a pound, and it sounded good. So I said, "Send me out a 10-foot (3-meter) log," expecting it to be this diameter or so. Well, he sent it out, and it was 20 inches (508 millimeters) in diameter at both ends, exactly the same, just like a rolling pin, you know.

Q. And very heavy.

Three thousand pounds. It came on a flatbed truck. They just unloaded it on the parking strip there and rolled it off on the dirt, and I cut it into three sections with the chain saw and rolled the sections back with no problem.... I've still got a big section there, just outside the door. It didn't have very good contrast in the grain, and I didn't work up very much of it. I never work up a whole log (at the same time).

Q. Do you coat the ends?

Yes, I coat the ends....I've got a bucket of paraffin over there, and sometimes I put it on a hot plate and melt it up and take an old paintbrush and cover the ends in paraffin. But I still have some commercially made end-grain

Bob used the paraffin in this pot for coating the ends of timber.

coating in the garage. I forget the name, but Burt Green gave it to me—he's the one who wrote that Selectorama book on hardwoods. Actually, his widow gave it to me—practically a five-gallon can of it. I've been using that ever since, and I still have practically a gallon of it. It's a sort of rubber solution in liquid form, and it dries clear and seals the end grain. Sometimes, I put dates on roughed-out bowls so I'll know how long they've been drying. That's all. I never weigh them. If I have whole log pieces, like when I get a whole load of black walnut (mostly salad bowl stock—sometimes, I'll get a whole tree, a log), well, then I'll cut it into 4-to-6-inch (102-to-152 millimeter) slabs and about 20-to-30 inches (508-to-762 millimeters) long. Just slice it up into reasonable lengths, load it on the truck, bring it in, and paraffin the ends. I don't coat the whole piece—just the ends.

Q. Are there any woods you would coat more than the ends? Like the pistachio— you were going to use the poly for that.

The pistachio has really thick sapwood, so even if it cracks on the surface, I would probably cut that sapwood off anyway, or turn it off. The important thing is to ensure it doesn't honeycomb on the inside.

Q. How do you use polyethylene glycol?

Well, I've got a tub of it over there, and I rough out a bowl and throw it in the tub.

Q. So the bowl is roughed out with equal thickness?

Yes, and I immerse it in the solution and leave it for about five days, at the most.

Q. Is it heated?

I don't heat it, but the solution...I just go by looks now. It used to be that when I'd make it up from scratch, I'd use six parts water and one part poly, and then I'd use hot water to get it to dissolve and so on. And then it will stay liquid from then on. But nowadays, if I want more volume, I might add a little poly and a lot of hot water because the water evaporates out, and the polyglycol stays. It's not cloudy, now it's black with age. The various woods I've used have stained the solution now, so it's sad-looking stuff. In fact, it occasionally gets a fungus on the surface of the polyglycol, and then I just take some hot water and stir it up and throw the piece in there and let it soak a few days. I don't try to get very much penetration. If it penetrates

one-sixteenth inch (1.5 millimeters), that's enough for me, so that I can turn it all off. I don't want any of the polyglycol in the wood, because you have a finishing problem then. If you get a complete penetration, for me, it slows down the drying on the surface of the wood, and it pulls moisture out of the wood inside and keeps the surface of the wood somewhat moist. (The late Ed) Moultrop (an architect-woodturner from Atlanta, Georgia) uses complete penetration. He keeps the wood in for 6 months or so, and he works with porous wood to start with. And so he's got a finish, and it's the only finish he uses, and he wouldn't tell me the finish. It's one of his secrets, and I give him a bad time about that. He said he's had all kinds of problems with the finish he uses, and he says it's so critical to get the right mixture. From what I gather, it's sort of an epoxy finish he uses on the bowl. He gets enough soaking and penetration that he doesn't get any movement problem at all. With the polyglycol, if you get complete penetration, the wood won't harden. It's the same as it was when it was growing. In order to get complete penetration, you have to work with green, wet wood. The wood needs to have a lot of moisture in it because it goes in and replaces the moisture in the wood. And then the wood is not any harder than when it was growing, and it never will harden. It's soft. That's another reason why I don't want to soak it all the way through. I want it to harden up a bit.

Q. So after you keep your bowl in the poly for about five days, you remove it and then you finish it?

I leave it in the unheated room here in the basement. I even put it here on the floor sometimes, if I'm very sure it's going to crack. And sometimes, it does—it just cracks anyhow, and I just throw it away.

Q. You want it to reach some equilibrium and still be moist?

Yes, the polyglycol pulls the moisture from the wood.

Q. Does it pull it from the air, too?

It pulls it from the air if it's a damp day. It also pulls it out of the wood.

Q. So when you're turning, you are taking this moisture off the wood?

It's not pulling it very fast, so you're not getting any honeycombing or anything like that. It slows down the drying process. I don't do a lot of drying with polyglycol. I had a 55-gallon drum of it, and I managed to sell all but a chunk of it that I have in the garage.

Q. Most of the woods you are working with are stable, and you know them well?

Occasionally, I'll get some local fruitwood. Most of the local fruitwood cracks. Almond, for instance, is very bad for cracking. Apple will crack badly, too.

Q. So you would use polyethylene glycol right from the start?

I just throw it in there as a precaution…. I get peach, a little cherry; once in a while, I'll get

some with a beautiful black marking in it, just like you took a paintbrush and made markings in it. But I haven't had any of that in a long time.

Q. Small stuff, though?

Yes.

Q. The repairs that you do, such as filling cracks…do you fill all cracks?

Oh yes, I'll fill exterior cracks before I'll do any more turning on the piece. In fact, I'll dig it out, all of the loose bark or anything I can. The inside, I don't care, because I'll turn that off. It's important to fix the exterior so it doesn't chip out in the turning process.

Q. Do you clean it out with a dentist's pick or something like that?

Yes, I have some dentist's tools I got from my Houston orthodontist. They have a little hook, and I just hook it out. Now, this one I probably won't clean out, because it won't chip out when I'm turning it. I'd rather do the cleaning after I have them turned to the thickness I want. That's when I do all of the repairs, usually. But I will do some repairs before turning in order to get them down to the thickness where I can do the repairs. I know (David) Ellsworth and (Hap) Sakwa use tape on the outside to hold their bowls together. Once in a great while, I do that. Usually, I can see where it's going to break out and I'll epoxy it right away.

Q. Most of the work you do is work other than burls?

Black walnut burl, California, 5½" x 12¾" (140mm x 324mm). Though Bob didn't use burls often, this bowl is a wonderful example of his results when he did use them.

I don't use burls a whole lot. I can't get too excited about burls. I have a stack of burls. In fact, I have two burls over there turned from the pile. I've had a pile of burls for ten to fifteen years. I don't like burls as much as the straighter-grained pieces. Like that sycamore burl over there...I spent two hours filling all those voids. And because that's going to be used as a salad bowl, it has to be free of voids.

Q. Tell me about the epoxy with which you fill voids.

I usually use the sanding dust and the slow-setting epoxy. Never use fast epoxy. For one thing, it doesn't dry to the proper hardness for sanding, and it stays a little gummy for finishing. It's also difficult to mix with a sanding dust, because it's starting to set up. With the slow-setting stuff, I can mess around getting the color I want. More often than not, I don't use the dust from the same wood to do the repair. I usually use a wood that is a little lighter in color, because the epoxy has a darkening effect on the wood.

Q. Same thing with ebony?

With ebony, it's a different story. I want the repair very dark. With ebony, I don't even use sanding dust. I use lampblack, which is just about as black as you can get. I have trouble getting lampblack, and I finally found a close friend of mine who had it, and he just gave me a bunch of it. It used to be available readily because all of the sidewalks used lampblack in the final surface. They wanted sort of a gray color. That's the code. But if you go down to a concrete place or a lumberyard, they've got some cheap substitute that is gritty and not the real lampblack anymore. Now I have a source of supply.

Ebony, Philippines, 4" x 6" (102mm x 152mm).

Q. The object is not to let the repair stand out?

In fact, quite often the cracks just disappear when you use this lampblack. You have to hunt around to find them again.

Q. You bring stuff back for repairs?

That one is going to be a problem because it's a light-colored wood, and I'm sure the repair is going to show, but there's nothing I can do. I have some whiting that I'll mix in with some of the lightest-colored wood I have and make it as light as possible.

Q. Do you save dust?

Occasionally I save dust, especially the light-colored woods, like birch and boxwood. I have ten to fifteen different dusts in little bottles.

Q. Did you ever get into any decorative coloring?

No, I've never done that. I have a bunch of colors here Frank Knox sent to me from New York. I've never used them.

Q. Over the years, you've belonged to the Wood Collectors Society. Did you belong for the access to different woods?

I occasionally found it was an excellent source of supply for wood. I bought out a wood collector in Los Angeles. I paid $800 for $10,000 worth of wood. I still have pieces of it.

For Bob Stocksdale, every log and plank was a discovery. Obviously, after forty or fifty years of working on a particular type of wood, he knew how to treat it before working it and how to apply a design from his turning vocabulary to it to bring out the best it had to offer. But sometimes, even his experienced hand was fooled, and he'd find the wood was unmanageable or the log rotten inside. The following provides some insight into the decisions Bob made and procedures he used in going from log to bowl—or woodstove.

Limiting Shape

I've limited the number of appropriate shapes already by cutting the plank on a 45-degree angle. I've limited it as far as quite a bit of the shape is involved. Some designs are a result of the figure in the plank. For example, for one piece, the shape evolved because when I got the plank, it was 10 feet (3 meters) long. There was this area, a certain spot that was more highly figured than the rest of the plank. And there were no flaws showing on the wood, but I saw there was nice figure showing on both sides of the plank. So down in Los Angeles, rather than have the plank cut up to take back in my truck, I just had the bowl sawed out. I had them cut the plank straight. I took that piece, and I sawed it round. It was a square piece of wood, and I tilted the table to saw it round.

Finding Bark Pockets

I can get some small bowls out of the lower part if I saw it on a bevel. I got enough bowls out of that area to pay for all the lumber. So then, I put it on the lathe and started turning, and down in this area here, I ran into bark pockets. They didn't show on either side of the timber. I kept turning away and found I couldn't get rid of them and decided I would pretty much have to live with them. And by that time, I had this shape. It was a little bigger base than this.

That happens more often than not. You'll run into flaws, and when you try to eliminate them, by that time, you've worked out a shape. And take advantage of the chunk of wood; use as much of the wood as possible. I'll start by trying to use the maximum size of the block. Like on this particular piece of ebony, it isn't giving me any problems—just one little crack since I started turning.

Selecting Wood for a Bowl

There are not very many varieties of eucalyptus—maybe 10 to 15 varieties here in the Bay Area—all cultured varieties. The most common is the blue gum. The tree itself has sort of a blue look to it, the foliage. That's the only thing I can figure. Most eucalyptus is called gum because of the oils that are in the leaves. It is not related to the southern gum. There are many houses with their interiors finished with southern gum. In fact, that wood over there looks exactly like southern gum. This wood, they would use for dinner plates—red gum.

I've always used the California black walnut in the sizes that I wanted for the salad bowls. I could get a little teak and some genuine mahogany in 16/4. By genuine, I mean Honduras. After I got out of the CO (conscientious objector)camp, I bought a lot more stock, and I got some Guatemala mahogany, which is harder and heavier than the Honduras mahogany, but not quite as hard as the Cuban. It's a good, hard, firm wood. I was able to get that in pretty-good-sized timbers. I got that in 6-by-12 inches (152-by-305 millimeters).

63

Bob began many of his bowls from a log. Each step of the way, he inspected the wood for defects and attractive highlights. The object was always to get as much out of the log as possible. Here, Bob cuts off the cracked end grain from a newly split log.

Indian Rosewood

One time, I got several hundred feet of 16/4 Indian rosewood at $1 a board foot. There was an outfit called Davis Hardwood. *(Author's note: The firm no longer exists.)* They got in 10,000 feet (3,048 meters) of 16/4 of India rosewood. It was stacked up over 10 feet (3 meters) high and 4 feet (1.2 meters) wide. They brought it in for furniture. I guess they brought it in because it was available, and they figured out who to sell it to after that. It was all in 4 feet (1.2 meters) wide 10 feet (3 meters)

high at least, and they called me in and said they had it. And I got a piece of chalk, and I looked at both ends of the boards. I couldn't see the planks' faces, and I put my X on them. I got probably a dozen planks from them. It was sitting outside. When they said they were going to move them inside, I told them to throw my pieces out and I would get them. I went back, and the owner said "I don't know how you did it, but every time we got to a FAS (first and second cuts—the highest grade) timber, it had

Next, he measures out the largest-diameter piece he can cut from the log.

With the log marked for potential bowl blanks, Bob slices it up.

These are the different-size blanks of usable wood from the original log.

64

your 'X' on the end of it." Just about a month, month and a half ago, I was up at the Crocker show, and a lady came back into the backroom and she had a salad bowl made from that pile of Indian rosewood. She thought that it might need some spit and polish, but all it needed was a little buffing with steel wool. I don't think she had ever used it much. It still had a price tag on the bottom. It was probably $30 to $35.

I would get some more exotic woods, but only in sawed boards for trays. I made a few decorative bowls out of little 2-by-8-inch (51-by-203-millimeter) pieces of exotic woods, like bubinga and padauk.

Bob marks the surface of the blank to identify the top of the bowl as a guide for cutting on the band saw.

These two views show the blank after Bob made an angled cut on the band saw to remove waste wood.

Decorative Bowls

I could get better, thicker pieces suitable for decorative bowls. That contact I had in Los Angeles, they had more flat boards of exotic woods than they had logs. They were the best source for the exotic stuff. Jerry Glaser was the one who found the English source for me. He established good contacts for me. Glaser was bringing it in for people like me. He just liked to buy wood. Of course, he never made any markup on it, he just sold it for his cost.

I don't try to keep stocks at any particular level. I guess if you took an inventory, I have 10 to 20 tons around. Maybe half of that is firewood. It's wood I've accumulated, people give it to me sometimes and think that it's valuable. Sometimes, it doesn't have good color. There's a tremendous amount of waste in larger logs. I cut them up with a chain saw, sometimes right on the spot where they are felled. Not with exotics—which are usually small logs. The exotics are never an unwieldy size.

I usually don't worry too much about surface checks, particularly on darker woods. Ebony, in particular, is easy to patch. Sometimes, I'll buy a whole log. I lived in England for a year in 1966 and 1967. While there, I hunted around at various places and accumulated 1½ tons of wood and shipped it back to the United States. One type of log I bought was pure speculation because no one had ever heard of it before. It came from India, and they had four logs of it.

This view shows the end grain of the log after cutting away waste wood from the top and the bottom of the log.

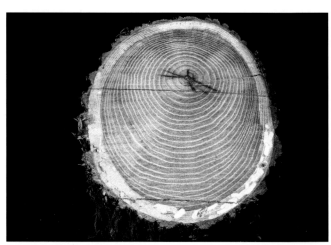

This log has marks for removing the top and bottom surface waste from the eventual bowl blank.

66

Bob follows the top surface guideline while cutting the blank on the band saw.

Bob uses the band saw to remove waste wood from the top and bottom surface of the eventual bowl blank.

Here is an unmarked log before identifying the best use of the wood and marking it for cutting.

Bob saws a taper on a round blank of walnut.

In the Shop:
Band Saw, Lathe, Turning Tools, & Techniques

Bob Stocksdale's workshop was not spacious in any sense of the word, but over the course of many years working there, he was able to find space for all of the tools he needed. This included a hulking 21-inch (533-millimeter) cast-iron band saw that Bob relied on second only to the lathe. We began our discussion with Bob's recollections on the origins of his band saw.

The Band Saw

That thing has quite a history. When I was on the farm in Indiana, when I was just a teenager and I dabbled in woodworking, you know. There was a furniture shop called Boracks Furniture located about 1½ miles away from me. It was the cheapest cheap furniture you can make. They used basswood for practically everything, and their main line was mostly little, cheap end tables that would sell for just a few dollars. They made them by the thousands. Well, they had this band saw in there they had used for Lord knows how long. In fact, the furniture factory burned down twice, and each time, they dug this band saw up from the ashes, replaced the bearings, put new rubber on the wheels, and they were back in business again. Finally, they decided that they ought to have a better band saw, so they bought a 36-inch (914-millimeters) model, and they put the old one out in the chicken house. I found out about it, and I

This is Bob's weathered 21-inch band saw.

Bob smooths the surface with a jointer before band sawing.

Bob rough cut all of his bowl blanks using the band saw.

A thick blank like this required two passes. Here, the sawing at the 90-degree angle has been completed.

conned the owner out of it. It was such a nuisance for me to go down there and use his band saw, so to get me out of his hair, he sold it to me for $10. I took it up to my shop and set it up. It had Babbitt bearings in both the top and bottom. I believe I had it in the CO (conscientious objector) camps, too.

It's hollow casting, and the frame is not all that heavy. It weighs something like 100 to 150 pounds if you take the wheels and everything off. There is a little bend, a curve, in the frame where it warped from going through the fires. You can still get the blade to run true.

A second pass was needed at a slight angle to create a conical shape.

Making Blades

Bob's band saw was a unique size with its 21-inch (533-millimeter) wheels. It was not unusual for craftsmen to make blades for even standard-size saws. The process of annealing, or softening, the ends of the blade to a certain color and brazing them together can be a frustrating exercise even for a skilled turner. The cost of a new, ready-to-use blade was and is less than the effort to make one out of a roll of blade stock. For Bob, I expect it was a case of self-reliance, economy, and the frustration that came out of having a commercial blade break when he needed it most.

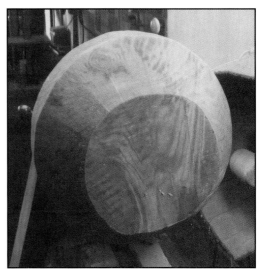

Removing excess wood on the band saw may seem like wasted effort, since cutting tools will remove it in relatively quick order. But, on a chunk of green wood, the type Bob often worked, it would make a significant difference.

The band saw is a 21 inches (533 millimeters). I always buy one-fourth inch (6 millimeters) blades, and I buy a 250-foot (76-meter) length box of blade stock and braze the blades up myself. I use silver-solder. I learned that at the little factory that I got the band saw from. They had a silver solder arrangement, and they showed me how to braze blade stock.

First, you bevel the ends of the blade back a little. You can do it on a grinder, and it doesn't matter if you overheat it a little, as long as you get the bevel on there. I have a little jig here that I made. I hold the ends of the blade with a hand clamp, and then heat it up with a hand torch. I put a little flux in the joint, and take a little tiny piece of silver solder, fit it in the joint, heat it until that melts, and use a pair of pliers to clamp down on it. After it cools down, you heat it up again until it is almost cherry red, and that anneals it enough so that it doesn't get brittle. I hardly ever have a joint break open. I used to have all kinds of trouble when the local tradesman's blade supplier would electric weld

them. They would reweld them for me when they broke, but it was a nuisance to take them back.

Four-tooth Blade

Bob relied on the band-saw cut for roughing out the bowl before mounting it on the lathe. Using a four-tooth blade for the operation resulted in speed, accuracy, and a smooth surface.

A four-tooth coarse blade is the only style I use. It's a skip tooth. I have, in the past, hit a nail or something on a new blade and taken the blade back to the shop where I bought it, and they will resharpen it for me. I found the resharpened blade is much sharper than the blade originally was. I save a resharpened blade for scoring

around the edge of my bowls. It does such a neat, clean job; sometimes I've even done bowls where I've scored around the entire side.

The upper blade has friction guides with a bearing wheel for thrust, and the under side operated for twenty years without a guide at all, but I found a guide made up of three ball bearings. Theoretically, it works great, but I find the ball bearings get gummed up, and I find the bearings not turning at all. I then have to clean them up. It does do a better job of sawing if you have lower guides.

Main Lathe

Bob's main lathe began life as a generic Delta 12-inch-swing, medium-duty machine and was modified over the years to suit his products. Like most of his machine tools, the lathe was braced, wedged, and bolted in place so it became an organic part of the workshop. While the swing was increased to support wider-diameter platters, it could not support large, heavy (wet) architectural bowl blanks. Every associated turning tool—from the tool rest to chucks to the tailstock—was tuned and adapted to Bob's direct approach to making bowls and plates.

A lot has happened in the twenty years since this interview took place. There is a myriad of professional lathes available for miniature through architectural turning. In 1987, the choices were limited leaving Bob and other pioneers to build their own lathes or modify a purchased one.

A close-up shows the band saw blade-etched outer surface of an ebony bowl.

First Lathe

Q. Which was your first lathe as a professional?

Actually, I acquired both of these Delta lathes at the same time. One of them I acquired when I was setting the shop up from an antique dealer here in town for whom I used to work. His name was Lew Mormon, Hudson Antiques. He had that spindle shaper too, and he sold them to me on the understanding I would do work for him, though not for free, whenever he needed it.

Q. When did the business about blocking up the lathe come about?

I think that happened shortly after I set up my shop. I always had this lathe blocked up. For twenty-five years, I had it blocked up with a

The headstock end of the lathe displays the countershaft below and the reversing switch at the top. The tool is an amalgamation of heavy iron, pillow blocks and bearings, and 2-by wood for spacers.

Bob's bowl count since 1979, which was tacked to a post against a wall in his workshop. According to the tick marks, Bob averaged about 300 bowls a year. Some years production was as low as 200.

couple of pieces of maple, and finally I decided it was going to be permanent, so I got those steel beams and put them under it. It made a difference because the bolts would eventually compress the maple, and I would find that the bolts would loosen up. I could use pieces with a diameter up to 18 inches (457 millimeters).

I got the big lathe probably in the late-1950s. I was driving up the road one day, and I saw that frame all welded up on the side of the road. It was made up of steel I-beams from a bridge. I could tell it had been welded up to make a lathe. It had no pulleys, no tailstock. It consisted of the ways, headstock, and was cut away there for the belt. There wasn't any shafting or anything on it. It was an unfinished lathe. I also knew who had done it. It was a fellow who owned a lot of acreage up in the hills, and his name was Judd Boynton. He was sort of a recluse up there. He dabbled in woodworking; he had it welded up, intending to make a lathe out of it, and he had put it out by the side of the road to keep the road from washing out. So I just hunted him up and asked him about it, and he said, "Yeah, you can have it, just give me a piece of wood." So, I gave him a piece of black walnut for it. I took it and put some shafting on it, some pulleys, motor, and so on, and about six to eight years ago, a fellow gave me a tailstock for it.

Q. Do you use it much?

I use the tailstock occasionally—for instance, when I'm finishing off the bottom of a large bowl.

Bob made this S-shaped tool rest with a curved end for supporting the turning tool deep in the hollow of the inside of a bowl blank.

S-shaped Tool Rests

The beginning of this portion of the interview starts with the end of a question about S-shaped tool rests for bowl turning. I had asked Bob for his thoughts on the manufactured tool rests and their shapes. In all of our discussions about tools, Bob's perspective was pure practicality. He was happy to buy a tool rather than make it, if it worked for him (the four-jaw chuck) and the price was right. If it was not available, he built it. He built one of his three lathes, tool rests, and band saw blades. Even when he found store-bought supplies, he would usually find a way to tweak them to make them work more efficiently.

My objection to commercially made S-shaped tool rests is the curves are too sharp.

Q. The ones that you have are made of mild steel?

Yes, a regular carbon steel, they're not hardened at all. That big one there, I had made up for me. The curve I did myself right on that lathe. I just took a blowtorch and heated it red-hot and took a heavy hammer and beat it in shape.

Pillow Block

Q. Explain the pillow block idea for the headstock of the lathe.

The shaft on it is a standard-ground shafting that you buy at a bearing supply company. It's standard 2 inch (51 millimeter) ground shafting—it comes that way. The Babbitt bearing next to the chuck is standard and it fits the ground shafting. I didn't have to machine either. I think it's one-sixteenth inch (1.5 millimeters) under 2 inches (51 millimeters), that shafting is, and the Babbitt bearing is the same size.

Q. Is that a thrust bearing on the end?

The end is a double-roller bearing, and it controls the endplay. It's a 1 inch (25 millimeter) bearing. It cost more than twice the cost of the Babbitt bearing, and it's only 1 inch (25 millimeter). I had

the shaft milled down to 1 inch (25 millimeters). I originally had a 1 inch (25 millimeters) shaft on that lathe, and so I had two double-roller bearings, and the 1 inch (25 millimeter) shaft whipped in the middle. It didn't work. It wasn't good enough.

Q. What did the whipping do? Would it make the bearings wear down?

Well, no, it just made your work flop. It was too limber in the center. I even put a lignum vitae bearing in the middle to take care of that whipping. Then, I had the top shaft milled out. They put standard South Bend lathe threads on it so I could use a standard South Bend lathe big chuck. I ran across that big chuck and bought it for $30. I got it from a widow of a woodworker, here in town, that I knew. She was getting rid of all of his tools, so I went up there and spotted that big chuck. It was a real great find because that thing cost like hell when new.

Q. This lathe is not bolted to the ground, and you use it as a finishing lathe, while the other two are bolted down?

Sometimes, like down at the Woodline tool store, they come and get that lathe and take it down for demonstrations because I prefer to use my own lathe if I can, because it has the jack-shaft and the reversing switch.

Here is Bob's complete tool kit for bowl turning.

The Reversing Switch

Q. Did the reversing switch happen early on too?

Yes.

Q. Why did you put it on?

I put it on mostly as an aid in sanding, see. When I have a tough piece of wood that is tough to sand, I will reverse the direction with each grit of sandpaper. If it's an easy wood to sand, then I won't reverse it until I get to the final sanding.

Q. And all of these reversing switches have silver contacts that you put on them?

Yes, sterling silver on the points.

Q. Were they pieces of sterling silver that you brazed on?

Yes, but I didn't even braze them. I just soldered them with an ordinary solder. I just took some sheet silver and cut out some tiny squares. It doesn't have to be thick silver, something like 24 gauge. I just used a solder iron. I put a little solder on one side of the silver and some solder on the point, and used the soldering iron to heat it and fuse it together.

Spring-loaded Switches

Q. The switches are spring-loaded, and you didn't have to change the settings inside, did you? They still make contact with the silver added?

No, after you get them on, just round the corners off with a file.

Q. You seem to have these lathes pretty much where you want them now. Is there anything wrong with them?

This small Delta lathe, for instance, is where I do most of my turning. It would be better if it had a heavier shaft in the headstock. Quite often, I have work that causes a little vibration problem because it's only a 1 inch (25 millimeter) shaft. It would be better if I had a bigger shaft like the Powermatic model (their best model) that has a 1½-inch (38-millimeter) shaft. The disadvantage with the Powermatic model is that you can't block it up to get the big swing that I like. It would be rather expensive and time-consuming to replace it.

Q. The lathe is bolted down, and you have a couple of rods to strengthen and give rigidity to the lathe while turning?

The feet are set in concrete, which eliminated the whip up there at the headstock. I often thought of replacing that pine plank with a piece of hardwood because the bolts mash into the wood, and you can't draw them up as tight. In fact, I just discovered a couple of days ago that this one leg is not fastened to the floor. The bolt pulled out of the concrete. But I didn't get any shake or anything out of it, so I guess it's been that way for years.

Main Cutting Tool

Bob's main cutting tool was a one-half inch gouge. The size and shape of this tool was very similar to the spindle gouge found in many standard sets. The channel down the center of the tool was shallow and the cutting edge was long and finger shaped, with the two corners ground back out of the way. When Bob began making bowls, there were no gouges specifically made for bowl turning, and resorting to scrapers was not an effective alternative. The long spindle-gouge bevel resulted in a shearing edge that could be dragged along the wood surface to shear and shape the inside or outside of the bowl. The corners of the blade were ground back to allow the shearing blade to take a deep cut without catching the turning wood. Unlike deeper U-shaped blades, the blade on Bob's spindle-gouge-shaped tool did not leave spirals in the surface. And in the hands of a master craftsman, this shearing cut left a burnished surface on all but the end grain of a bowl or platter and greatly reduced

An assortment of tools made by Jerry Glaser Tools for sale. The gold coating reduces friction on the tool rest and the wood. The metal handles are filled with shot to maintain balance while turning.

the amount of sanding needed to finish the piece. The discussion began with discussion about improvements possible in the making of woodturning gouges. We had been talking about this on the way into the shop and I began recording mid-conversation.

Jerry Glaser, an important figure in the improvements of turning tools, had been a friend of Bob's since 1959. As an amateur woodturner, Jerry was attracted to Bob's bowls when he first encountered them at a high-quality, modern furniture store, Frank Brothers, in Long Beach, California. The bowls were for sale in the store and accented the furniture pieces. One thing led to another, and Jerry's background as a machinist sparked a discussion on tools and the materials used to make them. Bob showed Jerry a scraper he had made out of M2 steel and said it would be great if he had a gouge made out of the same material. So, using an example of Bob's favorite gouge, Jerry made a half-dozen duplicates in M2 high-speed steel. Bob was ecstatic. The Rockwell hardness measured a solid 60R, and the resistance to heat, whether generated by the aluminum-oxide white grinding wheels or by rubbing against the highly resinous exotic woods, was a big improvement over the high-carbon Buck Brothers-style tools Bob had previously relied on. Jerry also made a 1-inch gouge according to Bob's design. He did not make high-speed steel replicas of Bob's scraper or parting tools. One other tool Jerry made for Bob was a blade-holding fixture to aid in maintaining the right angle while sharpening tools on the grinding wheel.

Over the years, their friendship continued, and Jerry acquired some of Bob's bowls and provided additional turning tools made out of newer and better alloys. These alloys included Crucible Particle Metallurgy (CPM) and M4. In the case of CPM10 and CPM15, Jerry was an innovator. He used a special, cryogenically treated metal with an altered crystalline structure to produce a material that would hold an edge longer than other materials.

The experimentation and innovation grew from Jerry Glaser Tools in the 1980s to today's Glaser HiTec, with materials supplied by Crucible. After years of running the business and supplying tool dealers globally, Jerry sold his company to Cryosteel Engineering and Technology in 2005.

Bob's one-half inch gouge was his main tool.

A view of the entire Stocksdale blade. After the first batch of prototypes, all succeeding blades were ground from nine-sixteenths inch (14mm) round bar stock.

Using Chromium

Q. Jerry was thinking about using chromium. Was it just on the inside?

Yeah, it's sort of a gold color. The first one cost him $75, but it didn't work. Another one looked as though he had dipped the entire end.

Q. Well, when did you begin using the M2 high-speed steel?

Jerry machined the first tools about ten to fifteen years ago out of round stock and sent it out, had it heat treated and it worked fine. Jerry also made a 1-inch gouge, and mounted those on a metal lathe, and they were made out of square stock. He milled the outside and inside.

Q. Before you had this stuff, what did you use?

I used whatever I could get—mostly Marples and Buck Brothers. I tried them all. One wasn't any better than the other. They were just carbon steel. I had real problems with turning some of the exotic woods with the carbon-steel tools. You could get a good edge, but it wouldn't stay. Some woods would turn the edge right over.

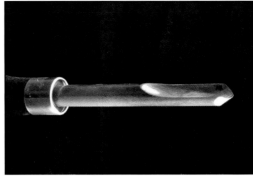

Bob's scraper was shaped and ground from heavy carbon-steel bar stock.

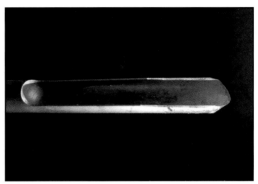

Bob's 1-inch gouge, shown here, was a tool he used occasionally. He relied on the one-half inch gouge for most work, even on the largest pieces.

This is the original model gouge Bob gave to Jerry Glaser to duplicate. Bob's one-half inch gouge was his main tool.

Here is the finished one-half inch gouge, manufactured by Jerry Glaser for sale to tool merchants.

Q. How did you arrive at the size for the gouge? It's one-half inch.

It's milled from a nine-sixteenths inch rod. But by the time you grind it, it ends up one-half inch.

Q. You use this for roughing- and finishing-type cuts?

Well, on smaller bowls, I use it for the whole process. If I'm doing a large bowl with a lot of wood to move out, I use that larger gouge to take most of the wood out. It saves a little time because it makes a bigger cut and doesn't get dull as quickly as the smaller one.

Q. How did the depth of the groove come about? Were you copying the depth of the spindle gouges that you were using?

No, I had never been satisfied with the curvature of the gouges on the market.

Q. They are all over the block. Some of them are shallow, and the bowl gouges probably would not work for your style of turning.

I hate long-and-strong tools. You have so much steel to grind away. My high-speed steel gouge is all that is necessary. Of course, if you're an amateur and aren't used to turning, or you are standing a long way from the wood, then the long and strong tool is okay.

Reluctant Teacher

Bob's reluctance to teach his turning methods never seemed strange to me. His main tools— the spindle gouge, skew scraper, and parting tool—were standard issue. But in order to use these tools to effectively and safely copy his process, each step in the preparation of the block and in his way of shaping it had to be followed. That meant removing wood with the band saw, drilling a depth-gauge guide hole, and coordinating the cutting with tool rest placement, cutting-edge angle, and hand/body movements. Only by following each step of the process could one hope to reduce the danger in approaching a fast-spinning piece of wood with a delicate-edged tool and achieve similar results.

Bob surfaces a bowl blank on the jointer.

Facing Off

Q. Do you use the jointer for facing off?

Yes, when I'm working with really rough stuff, I'll use the jointer. I'll use it more than you would think, especially when I'm making salad bowls, even sometimes when I'm making decorative bowls, too. For instance, this has a flaw here. Now I could use that jointer and get a tapered cut off here and eliminate that if I want to. On this one, I won't, but on some wood, I would eliminate the flaw, just by taking a tapered cut. With the jointer, I can do that pretty easily.

Q. Does that mean that the bowl will have a scalloped edge to it?

No, it will still be flat on top. You see, actually I take a tapered cut until I get rid of the flaw, and I take it off the base until it is parallel with the face. Then I band saw it out.

Q. So you use the jointer to make a smooth base on salad bowls where you want to finish the bottom before mounting it on the lathe?

Well, I never turn it in one operation. I always turn the outside of the bowl, screw the faceplate on the base of it, and then hollow it out.

Here, Bob sands and then separates a bowl with a pedestal from a waste block of wood.

Q. Is it common for you to use the jointer to face off the waste side before putting on the screw chuck?

Yes, you really need a good surface to use the screw chuck because if it's too irregular, the screw will pull out too easily—because it's the friction of the two flat surfaces that really holds it as much as anything. If it's too irregular, you will get a whip even though the chuck is tight. I only really try to get it flat where the chuck will seat.

Q. For the bottoms of the bowls where you have a pedestal, is it common for you to put it on the lathe and finish it off or use something like a sander to finish off the bottom?

I do make sure the bottom is flat: I check it with the straightedge, and on the salad bowls. The final thing I do is hit it with the two sanders, but that is after I plug up the screw holes.

Q. So one sander is coarse and the other is fine?

That's right.

Q. You've also put a reversing switch on your molder.

Yeah, that's important there because some of the cutters have to be operated in one direction, and some of them have to be operated in the other direction. All spindle shapers have reversing switches on them to start with. That's standard.

Bob usually drilled a depth-gauge hole in the middle of a deep bowl to serve as a guide to the eventual thickness while turning.

Bob flattens the bottom of his bowls after filling any screw holes.

No Vacuum System

Q. Did you ever use a vacuum system in here?

I have one for the sanders you see, and that's all. I've got the sanders rigged up so I can stick the vacuum on, but other than that, I don't need it. For the little bit of turning I do on those lathes, I just turn the little circulating fan on and wear a mask when I'm working on those lathes, too. But I don't use them enough to go to the bother of putting in a system or anything. This one has a good, sturdy exhaust fan on it, and I just blow the dust out onto the neighbors.

Q. Most of the stuff is done green?

About half, I'd say.

Q. So for the green stuff, you are getting thick shavings.

So, you don't have many dust problems with the roughing out on those.

Q. And then when you put them back on and do the finishing, you shoot the dust out, and then you would bring it over here to this lathe for the final sanding.

Yes, just for that little base area. I do a negligible amount of sanding over there.

Q. And the springs on the jackshaft, that's one thing I will have to remember.

I hardly ever use any other speeds. I think if I were building up a lathe from scratch, I wouldn't even buy those castings like they have. I would go to a regular bearing supply place and get double-roller bearings, or something like that, and pillow blocks, and make up a jackshaft with the same idea with the springs and so on. These are just bronze bearings, and they are not so great. Both of these lathes had jackshafts on them when I got them, so I use them.

Q. The Delta is a very popular lathe. There's a faceplate over there that has some dogs in it. Is that for finishing the bottoms?

I think I had a special job I wanted to mount in there. I don't remember what it was. I haven't used it since then. It's superfluous.

Have you seen this Grizzly chuck? That only cost $40. It is really good because the jaws are so wide. It's really a marvelous buy. I got this about six months ago. And they make a three-jaw chuck, geared, for $10 more—$50. And I think I'll buy one of those and try it.

Drill Press

Q. Do you use that drill press for any turning operations?

Oh yeah, I use that for every bowl I make. For the depth gauge, I just drill a hole in here and turn to the bottom of the hole. And I don't have to stop and measure it or anything. I turn the outside of the bowl first, and then I take it to the drill press, drill my depth hole, and mount it so I can hollow it out.

Q. So you turn the outside of the bowl with the little foot, and you make the little hollow in the foot and flip it over and put it on the chuck.

Before I put it on the chuck, I put it on the drill press because I have a bit I use.

Q. Is it a regular auger bit?

It's a regular auger bit, but it doesn't have threads, just a point, and I have a mark on the post of the drill press, which is one-half inch (13 millimeters) if I'm going all the way through. So, I can go up or down from that mark on the drill press. If I want it less than one-half inch (13 millimeters), I just raise it up past the mark a little, or if I want it more than one-half inch (13 millimeters), I can lower it.

Q. You mean lower the table of the drill press?

Of course, if it's a thick piece of wood, I will drop the table way down, do the first drill, and then raise it up to the mark. No measuring, no nothing. I always use the same bit. Many times, I use both hands and use the foot lever to steady the wood.

Q. I like it when the wood is unsteady and begins to spin around with the drill.

That happened to me not long ago. I had one hell of a time straightening up the bit again. It's still a little off but not enough to bother.

Q. I assume that you never had fluorescents lights.

For close work, I never want fluorescents. I have to have light close to where I'm working.

Elegant and Economical

Bob's cuts were elegant and economical. A case can always be made for using a deeper and wider tool to rough out the waste before making a series of finishing cuts to define the final shape and surface. But doing so would not have been in keeping with Bob's attention to the wood and how it changed with each cut. Hogging out wood quickly leaves a rough, fuzzy surface that is not easy to read. Besides, how much time is really saved, and for what purpose, if some interesting grain pattern is missed in the process?

Q. Let me ask you about tools. Once I heard you speak and you said the ultimate gouge that you would design would be very thin.

I think the Glazer one-half inch gouge is pretty close to it, and if I was redesigning that, I would have one-sixteenth inch (1.5 millimeters) less in the heel. I also object to this stopping here in the channel on the inside of the gouge shape. I want it to go all the way down. When I get this ground down to where the channel ends, it's about done. It's awkward to grind and hone when it's stubby. Just recently, the last batch of gouges that I got, they cut this milled part down about 2 inches (51 millimeters)—to what it used to be. I've registered my objections to that, but I don't know whether they'll listen to me or not. For most people, you see, it'll last them a lifetime anyway. They don't grind it down like that.

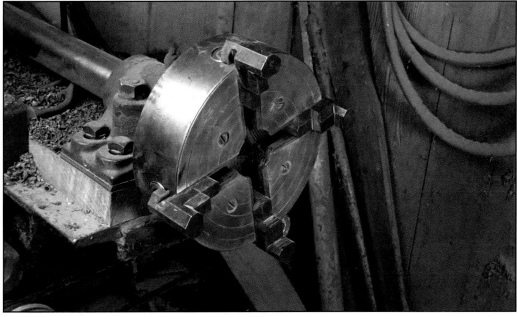

Bob's "old-school" four-jaw universal chuck.

Q. What about the length of the blade? Is that a good length for you?

I did design the length and the handle. Jerry would do the final fitting and sanding and putting on the ferrule. Jerry epoxies his ferrules on.

Q. When you designed this handle, you designed it to fit your hand?

Occasionally, I use the tool in one hand and support the tool and the bowl in the other hand. Then, I just hold it with the knob.

Q. Holding the bowl with the other hand is to counteract the flexing of the bowl near the end of the turning?

Sometimes, you get a little chatter, or vibration, and by supporting it with your hand, you can eliminate that.

Q. The support is on the other side of the cut exactly?

Yes. It's not very often that I do that, but once in a while.

Q. Is it mostly with softer woods?

Yes.

Q. What about the final thickness of the wood? Is there a standard thickness that you normally work down to that has developed over the years?

It depends a little on the shape and the wood. But I usually turn it down to a thickness that I like to look at. I could make them all thinner using the same process, but then they would get too fragile. I can make them look good without being too fragile.

Q. When did the use of the foot on the bottom of the bowls start, and why?

I've always made a foot on the base of the bowl, more or less, ever since I started making bowls, but I don't necessarily make a foot on the bottom of every bowl I make. A lot are designed without a foot. Whatever appeals to me—sometimes I make a foot, and sometimes I don't.

Q. Do you find yourself making a series of bowls of different woods and all with feet on them?

No. I mix them up.

The Thick Foot

Q. Did you initially start making the foot so that you would have someplace to hold the bowl on the headstock?

No. For ten or fifteen years, I didn't dream of using the three-jaw chuck even though I had it. Then, I was just using the screw and screwing into the base and leaving the base thick enough to take care of the screw. I wouldn't cut the thick foot off afterward. I would just drill out that screw hole and put a plug in there. Whenever I run across one of my bowls that has that, I can pretty well date it. At that time, when I was using that screw, I wasn't making many decorative bowls. I was mostly making salad bowls and trays. On trays, I would glue

a block of wood to the back of the wood with newsprint. Then, I would pop it off and sand off the glue with a belt sander. I still do that with the trays. The blocks behind the drill press are the ones I use.

When I want to make a tray, I'll go and look behind there and find a block that is about three-fourths of an inch (19 millimeters) too long so I have a new center to drill through. If I had a tray, for example, I would drill a new center and trim off the excess wood. Some of those blocks have six to eight centers. I use white glue—either Titebond or Elmer's white glue. Usually, I use hardwoods, but with the new screw (Glaser), I just use pine because it holds well enough. And then I sand it off.

Q. On this block with the screws in it, are you matching up the diameter of the disk? Would you do a large platter with this?

Yes, I've turned up to 24 inches (609 millimeters) on it. I mount this on the large four-jaw chuck. I have made platters up to 30 inches (762 millimeters). In that case, I usually screw them direct onto the lathe. I don't use the glue method. I screw direct into the base of the piece. On the waste side, I use the single screw only to hold it on the lathe.

Thuya, Morocco,
5⅝" x 4⅞"
(153mm x 124mm).

Sharp tools were an essential
part of Bob's turning techniques.

5
Sharpening:
Tools and Techniques

Bob Stocksdale's approach to sharpening was as straightforward as all of his other techniques. His high-speed turning tools were resistant to high heat caused by friction against a grinding wheel, so he used aluminum-oxide white wheels on a machinist's grinding machine for forming the bevel and cutting-edge shape. To remove the burr and smooth the edge, he used hand stones of various grades of fineness.

Q. Sharpening devices. Do you use that one (Japanese stone grinder) over there?

The Cutting Edge, a Japanese tool specialist located near here, had a special sale on them, so I bought one for myself and one for Sam Maloof. But I actually haven't used it any, except for butcher knives and a few things like that.

Q. Is that a wet wheel?

Yes, that's a wet wheel, and I've got an extra-coarse stone in it just in case I get a nick.

Q. I always had a problem with them because the stream of water would make it difficult to get the tool down against the stone, at least with the one I tried. I tried an early British one, and it is cool, but it didn't cut. It was like having an expensive birdbath.

That's why I got the coarse stone...because the 1000-grit stone was way too fine.

Q. So you've pretty much just used this grinder wheel here?

Yes, and the jointer blades I just send out to get them done. I use this for all of my turning tools always.

Q. And now that you have the white wheel, it's made your life a lot nicer?

I never had much problem with it.

Q. What about the hand sharpening you do after machine grinding?

I do it just enough to get the burr off.

Bob's grinding system was fitted with an aluminum-oxide white wheel.

90

Q. So you touch up the gouge near the end with the stone held flat against the bevel?

You see, it's hollow-ground, so I just hone it a little bit—just enough to flatten it—and then I do it on the inside of the gouge to get the burr off. That slipstone is the cheapest stone that Carborundum makes. It's the Fine No. 183 slipstone, and I keep it in paint thinner, not oil or water, and that keeps it clean. This one, I've used for about a year, and you can see it's getting a little hollow, but I've used them until they wore through. Usually, I drop them on the concrete and break them before that. But they don't have to be flat.

Q. You're working on such a small part of the blade anyway, you can use any part of the stone?

You can see this one has been dropped a couple of times, and the corners are knocked off.

2**To Turn the Perfect Wooden Bowl:** The Lifelong Quest of Bob Stocksdale

Sugar maple, Vermont, 1983,
4¼" x 5⅜" (108mm x 136mm).
Collection of Forrest L. Merrill.

The wood shavings fly when Bob begins to shape the

In Process:
Turning a Bowl

Bob Stocksdale's approach to bowl making was workmanlike and efficient. With each cut, new wood emerged and he often stopped to calculate the effect of continuing on the current path or altering the design. Sometimes there were surprises in the wood to deal with, and occasionally, the wood blank waited until he almost reached his preferred three sixteenths of an inch (5 millimeters) thickness before cracking. Such was the case with the blank of pistachio with which he challenged himself while I was there. The wood was hard, and the grain meandered about the surface with no indication of where the pith or bark may have once lived. He roughed out the outside and laughed knowingly when he saw the grain's pattern and felt the brittle and dense material resisting the gouge's edge.

After a half hour or so of shaping the outside and cutting wood from the inside of the bowl, Bob declared the blank a piece of firewood and was ready to throw it into the bin. Before doing so, he turned to me and said, "Here, why don't you finish it." And so I did, sort of. I took it home, finished the outside, left the knots and cracks as they were, and didn't touch the inside of the bowl at all.

The outside shape of the large, footed bowl is pure Stocksdale, but a shape I'd never seen before. The unfinished inside is alternately rough and unremarkable in some places, smooth and three-dimensional in others. For me, the cut surface is like a painter's brush strokes, evidence of the effort even a master exerts to wrest a shape from a block of wood, and a memento of that time in November 1987.

After observing Bob that day, here is what I can offer about his technique.

Shaping the Outside

As he always does, Bob begins by shaping the outside of the bowl. Using a one-half inch gouge, he shears away the wood using the middle of the side of the gouge to make the shearing cut.

It is important that the bottom be flat to draw the faceplate, which he will screw onto it, tightly against the surface (A). He flattens the bottom using the same shearing cut with the gouge (B–C).

Every cut is measured, and the speed and depth of the cut leads to a smooth surface in the shape intended (D–E).

A

B

C

D

E

Drilling to Depth

Bob uses a hole bored inside the bowl as a depth gauge. Markings on the drill press alert him to the depth of the cut so that he can account for the center spur in the auger that he uses for drilling this hole.

Bob developed his own method for drilling. With the freshly turned flat bottom of the bowl resting on the drill press table, and the table itself loosely attached to the drill press standard, he raises the bowl up into the turning drill (A). When he has nearly reached the last half-inch for the intended depth, he tightens the table on the drill press and uses the handle to advance the drill into the bowl (B–C).

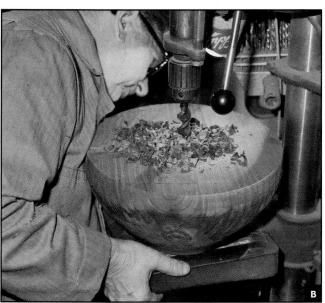

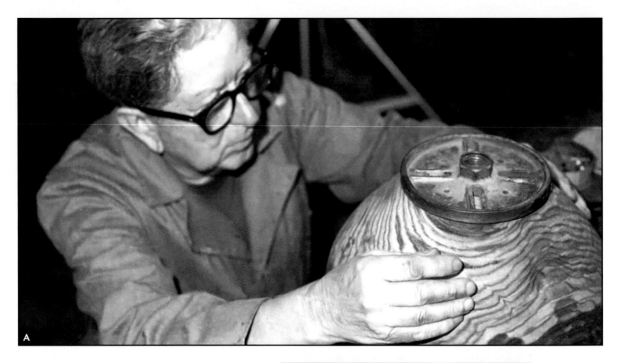

Attaching the Faceplate

Once the depth-gauge hole has been drilled,
it is time to attach the faceplate with machine
screws. Bob drills pilot holes and centers the
faceplate on the bottom of the bowl by eye and
attaches it with screws (A). A Yankee ratchet
screwdriver and some machine screws hold the
faceplate onto the bottom of the bowl blank (B).

The centering of the faceplate on the bottom of the bowl by eye is not always dead on, so a little cleanup on the outside is necessary (C–D) before proceeding on to the inside of the bowl (E–F).

Turning the Inside

Bob's approach to turning the inside of a bowl is practically the same for any size of bowl. Using the one-half inch gouge, he shears away wood with fluid strokes that follow the path of the eventual shape (A–D). He stops at times to check the thickness.

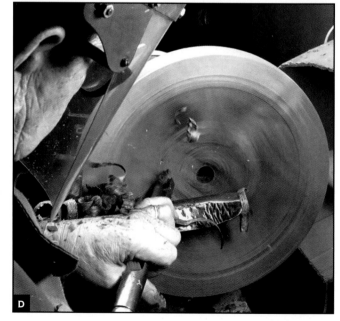

Since he has a depth boring to reach, the cut is not likely to catch an edge as it reaches the bottom (E–F). Once the shape has been roughed out with the gouge, all that is left to do is sand and finish (G–H).

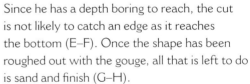

Turning the Inside for a Deeper Bowl

Here, Bob is hollowing out a bowl of a different design (A–G). Notice how he uses a caliper to check the wall's thickness (C).

Turning the Inside for a Shallow Bowl

Shallow bowls are cut in the same way as deeper bowls. With the homemade curved tool rest close to the surface of the wood, a series of shearing cuts is made with the one-half inch gouge (A–D). The consistency of the thickness of the bowl wall is tested along the way (B).

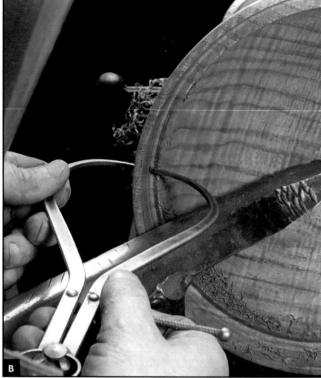

To Turn the Perfect Wooden Bowl: The Lifelong Quest of Bob Stocksdale

Turning a Pedestal

Bowls with pedestals are often held onto a faceplate with scrap wood and the support of the tailstock with a ball-bearing center. Here Bob cuts the pedestal away from the waste block with a parting tool (A).

Working with Natural Edges

Natural-edge bowls are cut the same as normal bowls, but the edge must be sanded by hand (A–E). A natural-edge bowl is essentially the same as a typical flat-topped bowl with two sections of the top cut away on the band saw. These two sections can catch the tool and sandpaper while rotating on the lathe.

To Turn the Perfect Wooden Bowl: The Lifelong Quest of Bob Stocksdale

Sanding

The outside and inside of the bowl are sanded with a power drill and sanding disks (A). The reversing switch on the lathe motor allows for sanding in both directions (B). This ensures a smooth surface because the wood grain tends to lie flat and can only be raised by reversing the direction or wetting the wood.

Final Steps

The final steps in the making of a Stocksdale bowl involve hollowing out the screw holes and gluing in plugs (A–B) and sanding the bottom flat on the belt sander when the glue has dried (C–D).

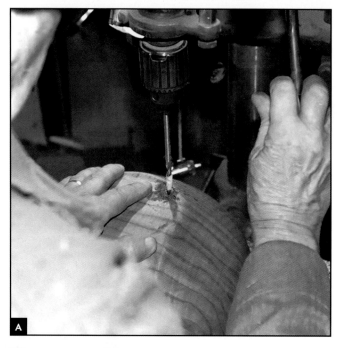

Bob sands the surface of a broad platter. The four-jaw
chuck grips the patter's turned foot.

In Process:
Turning a Platter

Sometimes Bob's techniques required dry and stable wood. At any one time, Bob had a dozen or more bowl blanks shaped and hollowed to a 1 inch (25 millimeter) wall thickness seasoning above the upstairs kitchen stove or immersed in polyethylene glycol. Bob marked the blanks above the stove with the date and periodically checks them for stability. When the blanks are ready, he then moves them on to the next step and final turning.

Shaping the Inside

These images show Bob using both the 1 inch and one-half inch gouges to remove waste from the inside of a bowl. The techniques are the same as those used for carving out the inside of a deep bowl. The long, curved side of the gouge, supported firmly by the tool rest, makes a shearing cut as it is drawn along the surface of the wood (A–B). The extra length and bulk of the 1-inch gouge makes cutting a curve a bit easier.

Shaping the Outside

Bob used a simple faceplate-mounted scrap block with a center screw for holding platters. Center screw holes from a 6-inch (152-millimeter) faceplate or three screw holes from a 3-inch (76-millimeter) faceplate were simply plugged up with wood plugs and sanded smooth. The rough surface of the waste-wood mounting block provided an additional gripping surface to support the hold of the center screw (C–G).

Sanding the Outside

The outside was always the first surface to be turned and sanded (H and J–M). Bob always used a straightedge to determine when the bottom surface was flat (I). This surface and the pedestal would be gripped by the four-jaw universal chuck for turning the inside of the platter. The final image shows the flat and short pedestal ready for mounting in the four-jaw chuck (M).

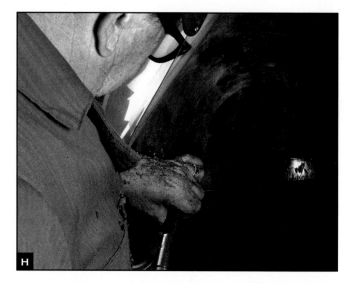

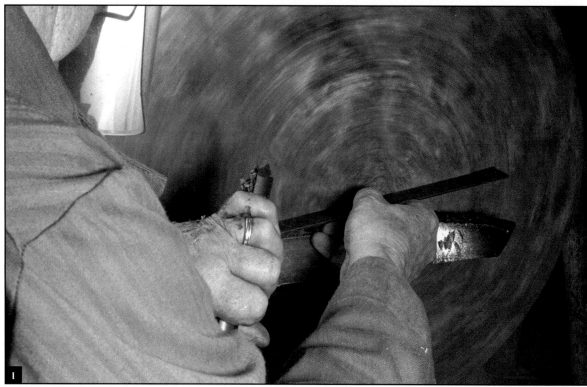

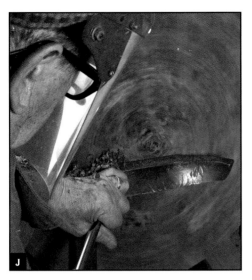

More Sanding

Achieving a silky-smooth surface on a platter, with the grain going from long grain to end grain and everything in between around the circumference, is serious business, and Bob employed every trick to make it possible. This often involved sanding with the lathe stopped, a variety of grits, and the use of motor-reversing switch (A–E). The last image shows the four-jaw chuck holding the platter (F). A firm grip was required to keep the wood from prying loose with each reversing-switch jolt.

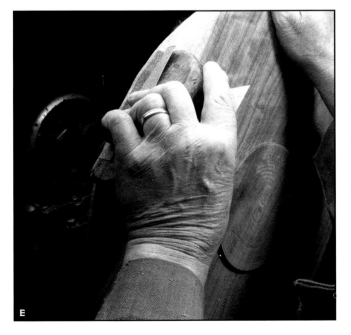

Cutting the Inside

Bob starts with shaping the outside of the platter and that then becomes the guide for the thickness of the final product. With the platter blank turned around and mounted on the chuck, the first thing to do is cut and measure the thickness of the wood with calipers (Figures A–D). Once the thickness of three-sixteenths of an inch (5 millimeters) or so is reached, the cutting in the middle of the blank can start in earnest (Figures E–G).

A

B

Cutting the Inside

When the bottom of the platter is reached, the surface is tested with the straightedge and flattened before overall sanding commences (H). Final sanding with the lathe running and stopped, and with the motor running clockwise and counter-clockwise, continues until the final surface finish is reached (Figures I–K).

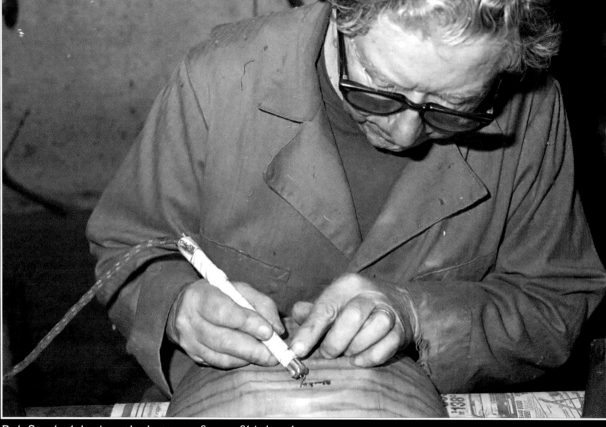
Bob Stocksdale signs the bottom of one of his bowls.

The Final Steps:
Sanding and Finishing

In the May 15, 1957 San Jose Evening News, Bob said he believed his success was due to the attention he pays to each piece he makes—from the initial selection of the wood to the final oiling. The satin-smooth finish Bob achieved on every bowl was a combination of understanding the fundamental characteristics of the grain and its hardness and applying just enough sanding to achieve his goal. He was one of the first to apply the reversing switch and drill-mounted sanding disc to remove tool marks on a turning. Using a power tool on fast spinning wood is not without its dangers, least of which is to the surface of the wood. For Bob, knowing when to move to the next grit, when to reverse direction to raise and sand grain, and when to work on an area by hand, were all part of the craft of making a beautiful bowl.

In this sequence, Bob sands bowls by hand and with a sanding disk assembly for a power drill.

Q. Let's talk a little about the sanding. On the outside of the bowls or on a broad bowl shape, do you do the disc sanding in both the inside and outside?

Yes, on a large-diameter bowl, I then sand the whole thing with the disc sander, outside and inside—both. In fact, on the big lathe, if I'm working on a large-diameter bowl, I don't even have the lathe running, I do it with the lathe stationary. I sand all the tool marks off. I just sand and turn the wood by hand until I get all of the tool marks off the inside and the outside of the bowl, and then I start the lathe and start with 36-grit garnet and work down to 220 grit. I've never used the self-sticking discs, I've always used the screw-on type. I always start with the 36 grit on the disc sander, with the bowl stopped, and then follow up with 60 grit by hand, with the lathe turning. Usually, I reverse with each grit of paper, especially with larger bowls. Not only does it do a little better job, but it is also physically a relief, so you don't get cramps standing in one position.

Q. Are those sanding blocks? The pads?

Yes, they're piano felt.

Q. So you take piano felt, and you glue it onto shaped blocks of wood?

Right now, this is for curves inside, especially on plates when you have a gentle curve all the way across. This is fantastic. I just wrap the paper around it. And I always use paper in a one-quarter sheet. I cut the paper into quarters, and I do that on the band saw, as a matter of fact. I stack up a whole bunch of paper in a number of grits and saw the whole works through with an old blade.

Q. It sharpens the blade at the same time, too?

Well, I throw the blade away then. I can saw 3 inches (76 millimeters) of paper at the same time.

Q. You have a couple of pads, one flatter than the other.

This one is flat, and the other is for curves. They are for sanding with the lathe turning. I use these mostly for trays and once in a while, for large bowls. In the decorative bowls, I don't ever try to use sanding blocks—I just use fingers.

Q. The sanding blocks work better than the discs?

The discs are okay, but you also get the circular rings from the discs. This does a better job of evening it out. I'm not opposed to other methods at all. These are just the methods I've grown up with and developed, and I haven't tried a lot of other methods.

While discussing sanding with Bob, I noticed the presence of gray/green oxidized sprinkler heads jutting out of the wall here and there about the shop. It surprised me, and I asked if they were real.

Q. You have a sprinkler system in here. Is it hooked up?

It's just on the water lines, and I have it all over the basement. I've had it ever since I put the shop in. Of course, it's not certified by the fire department but I'm sure they would be happy to see it.

I've never tested them (the sprinklers) out. The main reason I want one over there, and on the other side of the wall, is because I do lots of spraying there. There's a lot of lacquer there, and it would be a real hot spot if it ignited and the fire spread to the front steps. It's coated with lacquer underneath the front steps.

Bob's finishing room had bowls in different states of finishing and drying. On the floor are tubs for soaking salad bowls and logs.

Bob finished his salad bowls, often made of acacia, walnut, and teak, by soaking them in a tub of mineral oil for a few days so the wood was completely saturated. He would tell people to wash the bowls with soap and water when they were done using them. The oil would not allow the water to penetrate the wood. This oil would then bleed back to the surface.

Q. Tell me a little bit about finishing, how the bowls are finished. You spray your bowls?

Yes. I've got an old compressor there made out of an old refrigeration unit. I use a standard DeVilbiss sprayer, and I use a DuPont furniture lacquer. I don't use the sealer because the sealer is somewhat cloudy, and I don't like to use it. I build up the finish with clear gloss. I think I do thin it a little with a ten percent thinning direct from the can. If it were straight from the can, I would have to heat it a little, and that could lead to orange peel. By thinning it, I don't have to heat it. If you heat it, you can spray it a lot heavier.

Q. It's less viscous?

If it's an open-grained wood, you get a lot more orange peel, so it's better to put on two thin coats rather than one heavy coat.

Bob signed his bowls with an electric pen.

Q. And you don't fill the grain?

No. I don't fill the grain, even on open-grained woods like walnut. I don't care if the final finish shows the pores of the wood. I'm not after a piano finish or a Formica finish. I want the finish to still look like wood. So, I start with a couple of thin coats of thinned gloss, and then I sand it after two coats. I let it sit overnight so it hardens fairly well before the final finish. I put on a satin finish as the last coat. These coats get dust-free in about fifteen minutes usually, unless it's a deep bowl. The bottom area takes a little longer to set up. I usually wait a half hour between the two sprayings, and I spray the outside first and then set it on the shelf and spray where my thumb was. And the next operation is to do the inside, and I hold the base and spray the inside. In a couple of hours, I can get the coats on.

If you use more than one coat of the satin finish, you will get more of a cloudy finish, and you will not get the depth that you can if you use gloss coats followed by one coat of satin finish. After the final finish is put on, I don't do any sanding, polishing, or anything. It's done.

The sanding between coats is done on the lathe at very slow speed with 280-grit white paper. If it is a piece of stump wood that's quite porous, then I will use a coarser grit, such as 180, to cut a lot of the lacquer off where it has orange peeled, and I will probably put three coats on really opened-grained stuff to cut off the gloss.

Black walnut, California, 1973,
3½" x 8½" (86mm x 216mm).
From the Sam Maloof Collection.

Q. Do burls fall in that category?

No, burls finish easily. I don't have many
problems with them. It's the stump wood that's
porous. Anything that's below the ground is
porous. For that reason, I don't very often get
excited about it. I cut it at ground level, and
that's it.

**Q. And when you sand your pieces, you go
in both directions?**

Some types of wood do better sanded both
ways, but most do not need it. After sanding,
I'll dust it off with a tack rag or soft rag.

**Q. When do you put your name on it,
before or after you finish it?**

Before I put the finish on, after I've done the
final sanding, I put my name on.

Finishing wood is always a subject of great debate among professional and amateur woodturners. For Bob, after decades of turning and learning about the craft, mostly through trial and error, there was usually one way—the way that worked. This applied to seasoning wood, the use of cutting tools, and the proper finishing of salad and exotic wood bowls. But unlike most of the other techniques he developed for making the bowl, the finish had to work for the client—or his reputation would suffer.

Q. How do you finish your salad bowls?

The salad bowls I soak in mineral oil, not paraffin oil, which is not refined as much. There's two or three different viscosities that you can get, and I usually get the thinnest. I have a five-gallon bucket; I don't heat it. It lasts forever and never gets rancid. I let bowls sit for two to three days, depending on the wood. Teak, I usually leave in overnight—that's all. It's already oily. Walnut, I leave in for two to three days. Then, I wet it to raise the grain and sand it again. After it dries, the bowls can then be washed with soap and water.

I don't believe I've had any problem with the wood lending any flavor to the food. I had one customer who brought a walnut bowl back and traded it for mahogany because he didn't like the taste or odor of walnut. With cocobolo, I always put a lacquer finish on it. I don't make salad bowls out of it. I also put a lacquer finish on most of the rosewoods because of the oxidation problems if you put on an oil finish. Most woods, I find, will keep their color a lot better if you use a lacquer finish rather than an oil finish. I never use a lacquer finish on a bowl if I don't have to.

Yew, Oregon,
3¾" x 8¾" (95mm x 222mm).
From the Sam Maloof Collection.

Bob packed up shavings from his different woods for yarn
dyers. The shavings were used to create natural dyes.

The Business of Woodturning: Hard Work and Serendipity

The business of woodturning for Bob Stocksdale was personal. His direct relationship with collectors and their stories mirrored the intimate relationship he shared with his wood. The economy of motion that characterized his woodturning technique matched the simple economy that pervaded all parts of his life and clearly contributed to his survival as an artist. A survival that lasted over sixty-five years at the lathe!

As a retail merchant, he was cranky to unexpected intruders and charming to interested new collectors. His boyish grin was reserved for his wife, Kay, his friends, and the chance discovery of a long-forgotten exotic log under someone's garden shed. He didn't suffer fools easily and delighted in promoting fellow artists in whom he saw potential. He thought of himself as a craftsman, not an artist, and never glamorized his work.

All this was obvious as I watched Bob go through typical days moving from process to process intuitively, not robotically. In the end, I found myself envying the worn-in predictability and simplicity of it all.

Here, Bob speaks about making and selling turnings when he first started out.

Starting Out

When I started out, there wasn't anybody that I knew to talk with about doing turning. James Prestini had done some, Art Carpenter started about five to ten years after I began. When I started out, there was no competition. When I first brought some bowls down to Gump's in San Francisco, when I was at the Feather River camp for conscientious objectors, the store said it would take all that I made. They didn't know I was in CO camp. I had sent a group of bowls down to the buyer, and the buyer immediately wrote out an order: a dozen of these, and a dozen of those, and so on, and the total came to $900. It was a pretty staggering amount for me. I never did get around to filling that order. I never made any effort to. I went to see him and said I did one-of-a–kind work and didn't try to repeat on anything. Everything was controlled by the size of the piece of wood I had. I always made it as big as the raw material. I never glued up or anything like that.

Gump's was my main outlet for a number of years. They had other salad bowls, mostly the manufactured type with a lacquer finish that didn't last but a couple of years. They were made of myrtle wood, and they had some made down in Haiti out of mahogany. My pieces weren't a whole lot more expensive than the commercially made ones. I think my cheapest ones retailed for $25. The most expensive of the manufactured ones might have been $15 to $20. They had a section there at the store for just my bowls, whenever they had enough to fill up the section.

I was selling enough bowls early on to get by—only about ten percent out of the house, though. The wholesale price of the early stuff was so long ago I hardly remember. I didn't pay too much attention to how much they marked them up. Gump's always marked them up one hundred percent. I guess Fraser's in Berkeley did too.

As competition for salad bowls encroached, Bob started to focus on decorative bowls made from exotic woods. This shift in direction led to a need to find new sources of supply for these woods. At the time, Bob was married to his first wife, Nan, a teacher, and she had an opportunity to exchange classes for a year with a peer in England. Bob went along and used the opportunity to visit craftsmen and seek out wood suppliers in the United Kingdom and on the Continent.

Other turners started copying my turning styles. I think it was in the 1970s.

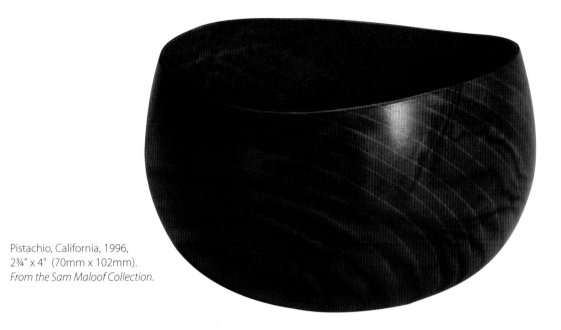

Pistachio, California, 1996,
2¾" x 4" (70mm x 102mm).
From the Sam Maloof Collection.

Pricing the Work

I guess in the early 1970s, I shifted from salad bowls to decorative bowls with exotic woods. I always enjoyed making the decorative bowls more than the salad bowls and trays. For that reason, I pushed that area. I showed them at shows and got good response.

In England, I didn't do any turning, but I visited many woodworkers, hunted for supply sources, and bought wood. We lived in Chiswick, near Hammersmith. We had a flat on the second floor, overlooking the Thames River. You could see a mile in each direction from the balcony of our place. It was nicely furnished with antiques.

I only visited one turning shop while in England. And that guy was kind of secretive about showing me around. He was an American, in fact. He and a bunch of women were grinding out bowls—like the myrtle wood shops in Oregon and Washington states.

When I visited Bob in 1987, he was in his prime as a collected artist and seemed cavalier about issues such as pricing and consignment. Times had certainly changed from his early days—from selling $25 salad bowls to selling $1,200 decorative bowls—but there was a core belief that seemed to guide his business philosophy from the very beginning. He expected appreciation for his handcrafted work. He expected it for the effort it represented, for his vision in identifying the form in the log, and for the value it brought to the owner. He liked selling to friends, and the best way to become a friend was to appreciate and buy his work.

Bob's ebony bowls, like this one, were some of his most beautiful and most expensive work.

As with most everything else, Bob had opinions and methods for every task in the shop. This included getting the right materials from the right person at the right price.

I use Styrofoam peanuts to fill up the voids, and many times, I use cheap carpet padding. The expensive kind is much too heavy, but the cheap kind is just a sheet of rubber three-fourths of an inch (19 millimeters) thick. I have a fellow who collects it for me; he lives near the place, and he just goes through the garbage every now and then. I nest bowls when I'm shipping more than one, and I place the foam between the bowls. The foam can't be too thin or the base of one bowl will make a mark on the inside of the other bowl, if there is too much pressure on it. I also use the plastic bubble stuff.

I never insure anything in fact. I send things first-class or priority mail, if I'm mailing it, and if it's UPS, I just get the $100 valuation. I've lost a few pieces, which were insured and then damaged, and they'll pay me off the wholesale

Macassar Ebony, 1980,
4" x 7¼" (102mm x 184mm).
From the Sam Maloof Collection.

To Turn the Perfect Wooden Bowl: The Lifelong Quest of Bob Stocksdale

Ebony, late-1970s. Large salad bowl 6½" x 13½" (165mm x 398mm); individual salad bowls, 1½" x 7" (38mm x 176mm).

Most of the shops now expect people to consign things to them. Twenty years ago, most of the stores bought outright. With the Snyderman Gallery in Philadelphia, I consign things to them for shows, and then I ask for the pieces back after the show because I can sell the pieces right here. And they thought I was mad at them or something like that. So writer Michael Stone was talking to me on the phone, and asked me if I was mad at the gallery. I said no, if they want to buy things, they can come right to my shop, but I don't want to consign them that far away from home. Then, I can put whatever price I want on them.

Pricing for retail and wholesale depends a lot on the bowl. A piece from a special piece of ebony, for instance, I would not wholesale. The price is $1,200, and you can mark it up to $2,400 or $5,000. If I know when buyers or collectors are coming, I'll just go in there and put prices on all of them, whatever I want for the pieces. Ordinarily I don't have prices on the bowls on the shelves.

If it's a major show, like when my wife, Kay Sekimachi, and I have a show together. We'll display twenty-five to thirty pieces. I will price them, and I expect to sell many pieces. I might put (the $1,200 ebony piece) in it, but it is doubtful. The price would be too high on that. What I will probably put in is a smaller piece of this piece of wood, like that one, which is going in a show at $500.

price on them, but they won't give me back the pieces. I'd just as soon have them back so I can repair them, 'cause I can usually repair them to where they don't show the damaged spot at all. I never have any losses in that respect. I'm very careless about the requirements of a gallery for insurance and so on. In fact, the Arts and Crafts Co-op here, is the only place I will consign things. I like to help the co-op out and take care of customers I used to have here in Berkeley who bought from Fraser's up on Telegraph when they were in business. I just take them down there and leave them. I don't get any consignment sheet or anything, so if they're stolen, I don't even miss them.

I prefer to sell the special stuff on my own. I find that I sell more of the expensive pieces here than the less expensive ones. So why consign them?

The decorative trays are not expensive, they're mostly $25 to $75. Of course, there's one over there for $750, but it's thuya burl from Morocco, and it has $600 worth of veneer in it, if it was cut into veneer. I occasionally make very large ones and I get a couple of hundred dollars, mostly because it is a large piece. It's easy to make on the large lathe. I can make one of those in a half-day, but of course, getting the wood is a problem too. But I have a good stock of the wood and a good source of supply. I've got a friend who does slabbing of woods. He borrows my chain saw occasionally. I just tell him I need a piece of wood so big, and he'll dig it up for me.

I rarely ever consider the time involved in making a bowl when it comes to pricing it. It's all in the grain of a piece of wood and the rarity of it that determines the price. They might start in price with $500 and up. It all depends on whether I can replace the piece of wood easily or not. I sell quite a few salad bowls here, but I take quite a few salad bowls up to the Arts and Crafts Co-op. I always see that they have at least one in stock. Every salad bowl has a set of salad servers included in the price.

So the middle-range stuff, such as the $350 ebony bowl, is the type that sells best through the galleries. For example, this $1,200 ebony bowl—ten years ago, it would have cost $750. I made one, more than ten years ago, similar to that—maybe 12 inches (305 millimeters) rather than 13½ inches (398 millimeters)—and I sold it for $750. It was a piece of ebony that only cost me around sixty-six cents a pound to start with. I got it at Penberthy Lumber in Los Angeles. It was a huge piece of ebony. There, for the price of the piece, because I knew I could get more ebony, I only asked $750 for it. Now, I can't get any more of it. I tried to buy the bowl back from the guy, but he wouldn't sell it. I probably wouldn't have asked $1,200 for it back then.

As an established artisan, Bob Stocksdale sold directly to collectors from his shop. He welcomed, but did not rely on, selected advertisers or retailers promoting his work, and that gave him a lot of leverage to control his own cash flow and maintain the integrity of his brand. Bob seemed to cultivate his flinty character as part of his business identity and perhaps as a defense mechanism for his independent lifestyle. However, in the early days, his independence was the result of his craftwork, his first wife's, Nan's, teaching career, and income from some rental property he bought in Berkeley.

I found I was paying all my bills, I wasn't in debt. Most of the shops were paying me on time. I cut out the ones that didn't.

Koa, Hawaii, 1982,
4¼" x 6¾" (108mm x 171mm).
From the Sam Maloof Collection.

Making Furniture

Bob only made furniture while working in the factories near his hometown as a boy. Once he began making bowls and platters, he never returned to furniture making. I asked him about this, and he confirmed it, with exceptions.

I haven't made furniture since I was young. Once in a while, someone will come along with a custom turning job that is sort of a challenge, and I'll do it but I usually send them to someone else. I do some things for around the house. Someday, I'm going to talk Kay into letting me make a couple of stools for her studio. The stools that she's got up there are worse than the ones I've got here in the shop. She keeps putting me off. Making furniture, I wouldn't earn what I can making bowls. One job I started doing twenty-five to thirty years ago, and I still do it once-a-year, is making a little stand for a

vacuum gauge, called a McLeod gauge. It's a very accurate gauge. The company is located here in town and I've known them since the year one. They asked me to make these bases, and it didn't involve a whole lot of work. They didn't sell a lot of them. They sell now for $250. There isn't a big demand for vacuum gauges that accurate. I said I could do it. Another reason I decided to do it was because it gave me a chance to use the spindle shaper, which I love. There's a lot of shaper work on it. I've been doing those ever since. They've increased sales. I used to do ten a year, and now I do fifty a year. I can do them in a week. I can get $1,000 for the fifty. I purchase the wood for a very reasonable price. To finish them, I use a sanding sealer first followed by one coat of gloss and one coat of matte. It takes a whole day to put the lacquer on them. I spray them.

Bob's flinty side could turn on a dime to a charming and generous personality. He would sometimes go out of his way for a fellow craftsperson. Sometimes, the effort would result in little gain, as in his ongoing relationship with yarn dyers told below.

This woman wrote a book on the vegetable dyeing of yarn. She ran tests on the different woods and then used my name in the book as a source of supply for the shavings. I've known her for years, and I said it would be okay. People have written to me for twenty years. I still get letters, and the book is still in print. I have sacks of shavings over there. It's kind of a nuisance. I don't make any money on it, even at $3 a pound for shavings. I lay out a big piece of plastic and then sack them up. Sometimes, if I get a request for a particular wood, I will have to tool up and make a bowl out of that wood to fill the order.

James Prestini

James Prestini is often acknowledged as the biggest influence on Bob's bowl making. Bob admitted to being influenced by his work. That influence may be most evident in the thinness of the bowl walls and the overall elegance of the shape. But the strongest direct influence is clearly the oriental art Bob saw at the Brundage Collection at the de Young Museum in San Francisco.

Over the years, I exchanged correspondence with Prestini and enjoyed his abstract musings on craft, art, and the people who do both. Although he lived only a few blocks from Bob, they hardly

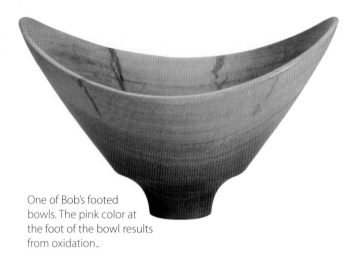

One of Bob's footed bowls. The pink color at the foot of the bowl results from oxidation..

ever met or talked on the phone. They were from two different worlds. Prestini was a professor of architecture at the University of California, Berkeley, and used bowl forms at one point in his career to apply his abstract design ideas. Form was usually most important to him, and grain and color were something to be neutralized. By contrast, Bob may never have thought of design in the abstract; rather, he was a craftsman who celebrated grain and form together as a product of his personal expression.

As far as design influences are concerned, I guess Prestini sort of inspired me to keep things simple and don't make them too bulky looking and so on. But if you analyze his stuff, you see that they were all one shape. And then I've always enjoyed going over to the Brundage College at the Asian Art Museum and the

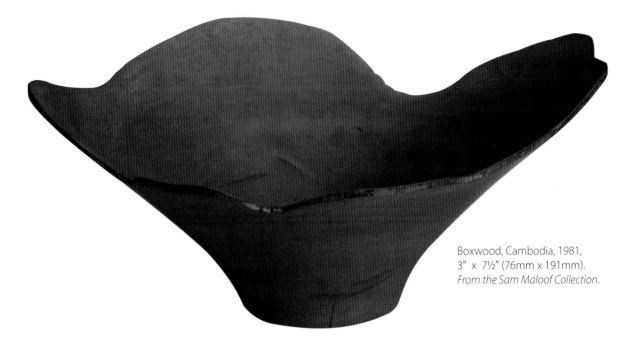

Boxwood, Cambodia, 1981,
3" x 7½" (76mm x 191mm).
From the Sam Maloof Collection.

Brundage Collection of Oriental Art to view all of the Japanese and Chinese decorative bowls. I found out *they were copying my shapes 5,000 years ago*. I began using a foot on my bowls around twenty to twenty-five years ago, I guess.

Trade shows, conferences, and symposia, for Bob, were an opportunity to travel and meet with peers. The gregarious side of his nature could be set loose, and he could share his day-to-day experiences with true fellow travelers. It was at one such event, years earlier, that he had met Sam Maloof, and their friendship had begun. Later in life, as his work became celebrated nationally, he and Kay traveled often to receive honors for a lifetime in craft.

The "Living Treasure" show is in Sacramento. Art Carpenter, Sam Maloof, and I are the three woodworkers. We have ten pieces each displayed up there. They gave us a framed resolution and five copies of the show catalog from the show. In fact, it's not a fantastic show. Eighteen craftsmen were selected. Years ago, there was the Designer Craftsmen of California. That was made up of Bay Area craftsmen. There wasn't any guild that we all belonged to back thirty years ago.

I did very few craft fairs. Years and years ago, I would do the San Francisco art festival. I also did the Berkeley art festival. I also did some demonstrating in Fraser's store window. That was the time I built a mound of layered shavings while turning. I knew that was happening, so I

Cocobolo, Nicaragua,
3½ x 5½ (86mm x 140mm)
From the Jerry Glaser Collection.

kept changing the woods so that would happen. It was quite a showstopper.

There was a designer group here in the Bay Area—Craftsmen of California—and that is the place that I first met Kay. She was a member but didn't attend the meetings. Whenever we would have a show, she would put things in the show, and that's when we would meet. That was in the 1960s. The purpose of the group was mostly social, to visit. We had group shows, and the group finally opened our own shop at Cliff House in San Francisco. We operated that for a few years. I sold quite a few things there, but it was a time-consuming thing because we had to do our work there in the store. There was a Playland, a big amusement park, at the beach. It was close to Cliff House. It was in existence for fifty or one hundred years, a long time. The owner of the Cliff House

and Playland stopped into the shop once, and he said, "Say, we've got some hardwood down there in the yard. It's Lignum Vitae or rosewood or something. I don't know what it is. We used to make the balls for the Skee-ball machine (with it.). It's been there for ages. You can have it if you want." So, I went there and looked at it. Here, it was all cocobolo, and there was over a ton of it. All of it was weather-beaten. The sapwood was completely rotted off the outside. I made him a couple of bowls and took them over to him. He was delighted.

Honey locust, Indiana, 1983,
2⅞" x 6½" (73mm x 165mm).
From the Sam Maloof Collection.

Teaching and Apprentices

I asked Bob about teaching and taking on apprentices, but he said he'd had very few inquiries over the years. Some craftsmen who had already achieved some modest local renown were welcomed and friendships were formed.

I've had friends come in and want to do work of their own. But I didn't let them stay too long. I've found that my production drops about fifty percent when I have someone else in the shop, no matter what they do. I decided that if I couldn't make a living at it during a forty-hour week, then I had better hunt something else up to do. I think most of the injuries in the shop are when people get tired and have worked too long. I've still got ten fingers. If you stop right in the middle of a bowl, when it gets really interesting, you're anxious to get back, and it's not a drudge. I always watch the clock when it gets to quitting time.

Jerry Glaser was an engineer and woodturning enthusiast who became one of Bob's closest friends. He made many tool prototypes for Bob, using state-of-the-art high-speed-steel stock shaped on high-tech grinders in his company's machine shop. Jerry is now retired and has sold his tool-making company. Bob liked to recount the following story about a boondoggle he and Jerry took to Germany in search of special timber.

When Jerry and I went to a timber merchant in Germany who dealt with woods for the musical instrument industry, we were talking about ebony, and the fellow said, "I've got a real bargain on ebony piano keys. I've got 1,700 in a unit here, and the piano industry buys them by the 100,000s, and they won't even talk to me about a box of 1,700. I've had them for a couple of years, and I'll make you a good price for them." He wasn't quoting prices at all at the time, but I insisted that he give me a price. After twenty minutes, he came back and said "Fifteen cents apiece." I said, "I'll take them all." It came to $285 for the 1,700 of them. I bought them all and six months later, they came into Los Angeles with the rest of the wood. I didn't know just what I would do with them. I was a member of the International Wood Collectors Society, so I thought I would do a favor to the members and sell off the pieces to those who just wanted a little piece of ebony. So, I put a notice in the bulletin that goes out every month to the members and said I had these piano keys that were 3¾ inches long and three-fourths of an inch square. They made a mistake and said they were 33¾ inches long

Unfinished bowls by Kay and Bob stand side by side in 1984.

and three-fourths of an inch square. I decided I would sell them for twenty cents a piece plus postage. Damn near every member wrote from all over the world. I got letters from Australia, New Zealand. I had to write back to them to make the correction because it took two months to make a correction in the bulletin. By that time, everyone had written to me or phoned me on the telephone. A lot of them called on the telephone. Most of them wanted them anyway. Finally, I decided I would have to limit the sales to a hundred piano keys to one individual. I had to pack and send them all. Very time-consuming.

For years, I had been providing Sam Maloof with plugs for his furniture. I used to have some darker ebony I made bowls out of. And I'd tool up the drill press with the plug cutter and turn the outside of the bowl, and then I'd take the plug cutter and cut plugs out of the inside of the bowl. It would take a couple of hours to do, but I made many plugs for him. They were all face grain. I never did end-grain plugs for him—he didn't want them. Then, I got these piano keys, and I figured they would make good plugs, so I didn't sell all I had.

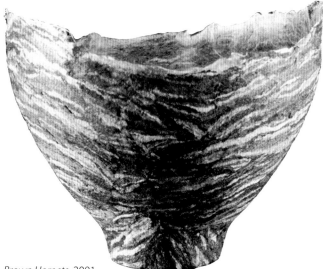

Brown Hornets, 2001,
4" x 4¾" x 4¾" (102mm x 120mm x 120mm),
Hornet's-nest paper, Kozo. *Photo by Richard Sargent.*

Collaborating with Kay

Bob's serendipitous collaboration with Kay on paper bowls is illustrated and told in "Origins of the Paper Bowls Shown at 'Marriage in Form'" on page 17. Kay's magical woven forms decorated the high-ceilinged walls of the house they shared together. They dwarfed even Bob's largest bowls and seemed to stand in stark contrast to their obvious practicality. Bob delighted in telling visitors Kay was the true artist there. If Bob was more renowned than Kay, it was only due to the cyclical popularity of weaving and wood and not to their mutually recognized accomplishments.

Kay's paper bowls sell very well. She has never in all of her weaving life made anything specifically to sell, with the possible exception of some place mats and napkins she has done. Since she has gotten a reputation, she never makes any effort to make anything to sell. It's strictly an experiment to see if she can do something or not. It turns out people want the paper bowls, and that's a surprise. She can't get over the fact people want to buy them. I keep telling her she never has to make anything to sell because I can make enough money here to live on, and we have enough other income, too, so we don't have to crack our tails to make things to sell. If she wants to experiment, great.

Paper Bowl, 1989,
3¼" x 6" (82mm x 152mm),
Japanese handmade papers, blue patterned papers.
Photographer: Unknown.

Bob's Collectors

Bob seemed to have personal relationships with many of his collectors. Collectors would often stop by the shop to see what was around and leave with a new piece. In the context of the California lifestyle, a hotbed for eccentrics and craftspeople, it seemed perfectly natural for relationships between artists and collectors to be informal and persistent. Over the years, I have come to believe that this local, eccentric support was the essential ingredient that allowed Bob to not just survive, but to thrive. Life would have been much different if he had remained in Huntington, Indiana, and not received the daily support of this local culture.

In 1959, Bob Anderson bought the first bowl for his collection, and he continued into the 1960s. A lot of them are flat trays, but he does have some beautiful decorative bowls, too. I can take you up there; it is quite an adventure. He's sort of a recluse. He's a bachelor, and he has a small machine shop in his basement, and that's how he makes his money. He grinds out parts for IBM and big outlets—small parts like a screw, a special screw, something like that. He has a couple of turret lathes. They may want only a couple of hundred or something, and he will make them. There's another fellow here in town who collects crafts, especially ceramics. He owns pieces by Lucy Rie, Hamada, Bernard Leach, and so on. So, he started collecting my things, and he has forty to fifty pieces.

I would call them and tell the people who collected my works if I had something very unusual, because I knew what they wanted. Anderson, for example, was looking to buy nice pieces, sort of an investment, I guess, if I had a very choice grain or something like that. The other collector was sort of a real-estate tycoon, and at one time, he owned a whole city block of residences here in Berkeley just a half-mile away from here. He's easily a multimillionaire, and he never has to worry about where the next dollar is coming from. He likes to keep it quiet when he buys things. June Swartz is an enamelist, and we have a bunch of her things upstairs. She had a show in the city, and he went over and bought half of the show—right off. And her things are expensive. He bought that as an investment.

Collectors got in touch with me in different ways. One collector bought a bowl at a show at the Museum of Modern Art in San Francisco. I had to contact him because the bowl was already sold and I borrowed it back for the Crocker show. Another collector found me through Fraser's. Probably bought a few pieces there, and then he was collecting many ceramists who I knew, and they probably talked to him about my work.

Masur birch, Russia, 1992. Different views of this bowl show the tree's pith, which is translucent on both sides of the bowl, and Bob's signature on the bottom.

There are national collectors, and they were written up in *Craft Horizons* magazine. They don't have many of my pieces. They recently wrote to me and listed the pieces that they had, and I wrote to them and said they didn't have a good cross section of my work. And I told them I should send them some pieces for them to select.

My biggest collector is in La Jolla, California. He saw my things in a shop there in La Jolla called Gallery 8. He would buy my things in that shop quite often. I finally did have contact with him because he was interested in getting better pieces, and I wouldn't wholesale the better pieces. He told the shop he was interested, and they told me, and so they gave him my name and address. I sold hundreds of pieces to him. He's easy got two hundred pieces. I don't know how much dollar-wise—$25,000 to $30,000, I expect. At least that. That's the biggest collection I know of. I guess he began collecting in the mid-1960s.

Neither one of the collectors in Berkeley have bought very much in the last ten years. Anderson came down six months or so ago and fell in love with one of the bowls on the shelves. He just about fell on the floor when he found out the price. "Well, I've got to have it. Can I pay you by the month?" So he did. On the other hand, I introduced him to another collector, and it turned out that they were both frequently eating in the same restaurant. Both went out for their meals, and they were both eating in the same restaurant. They somehow never became acquainted with each other. One time, they were both here in the shop. Forrest Merrill was always interested in getting a little tamo wood plate, and Anderson had two of the 10-by-¾ inch (254-by-19 millimeter) tamo plates, and Anderson was willing to sell. He charged him $200. I had originally charged him $20, I think.

From Blank to Bowl in Pistachio.

A

B

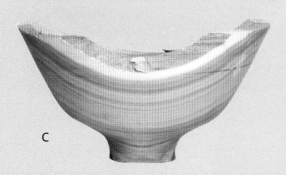

C

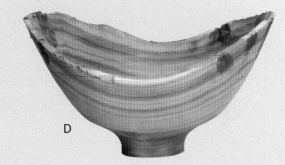

D

Shots of the stages from blank to bowl in Pink Ivory from Zululand. The stages include sawing and splitting a wedge-shaped section from the log (A); roughing out, at an angle, the outside shape of the bowl (B); drilling a depth guide with a drill press (C); and turning the piece inside and out to a finished form (D). The wood at the cutting and early turning stages exhibits a golden color that will eventually turn lighter near the sap and pinker near the heart (E). The finished piece is displayed on page 28.

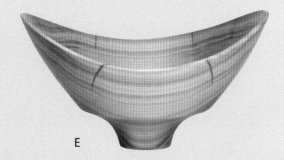

E

Prices have gone up gradually. What pushed prices up was the exotic grain pattern I would occasionally run across. I would boost the price on that particular bowl. Even now, I have bowls over there that I'll sell for $75, with the same shape and size of bowls costing $750. It was in the early 1970s that I started to get more exotic woods.

Shedua, Africa,
¾" x 15¾" (19mm x 400mm).

Goncalo albes, Brazil,
¾" x 11½" (19mm x 292mm).

To Turn the Perfect Wooden Bowl: The Lifelong Quest of Bob Stocksdale

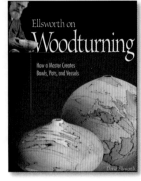
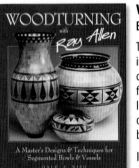

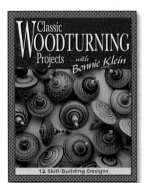